MW00328412

We all face painful challenges in our lives, and sometimes it takes someone who is willing to share their own hurt before we can make sense of our own. Rebekah opens up her heart and her life with the kind of beautiful vulnerability that will make you ache and reveal to you a path to healing for your own difficult stories.

CANDACE CAMERON BURE, actress, producer, entrepreneur, and *New York Times* bestselling author

In today's weary world, the reminder that we can live a beautiful, resilient life—not without struggle and hardship, but in and through it—shines through every word of this book. Rebekah Lyons writes with a wisdom, vulnerability, and compassion that come only through facing life with resilience. She offers us great hope and gently guides us to orient our hearts toward the God who has all things in his hands.

KORIE ROBERTSON, author of *Strong and Kind* and star of A&E's *Duck Dynasty*

I needed this book, and I'm sure you do too! For those of us who have been bumped and bruised along the way (that's everyone, right?), this book offers wisdom and a road map for building a life that can weather storms in grace and love. I'm so thankful for Rebekah and her story that leads the way for us.

JEFFERSON BETHKE, *New York Times* bestselling author of *Take Back Your Family*

I have personally watched Rebekah Lyons live this message. The words in this book come from a resilient life. She and Gabe know difficulty, and they also know joy. In a world that is falling apart at the seams, Rebekah will give you handles to build a thriving, strong faith.

JENNIE ALLEN, *New York Times* bestselling author of *Get Out of Your Head*

To become durable—to develop resilience—is to live into the infinite depth of eternity that God has set in our hearts. It is with this vision of the ever-deepening, eternal kingdom of God in her sights that Rebekah Lyons has provided us a wise, accessible offering that leads us not merely to survive but to flourish. Read this expectantly and with hope, but not without the willingness to do the necessary work that God longs to join us in as we become what God imagined before the foundation of the world.

CURT THOMPSON, MD, author of *The Soul of Desire*,
The Soul of Shame, and *The Deepest Place*

If life has left you weary and overwhelmed, don't wait a single second to jump into these hope-filled pages! With compassion and clarity, Rebekah Lyons shows the path forward through life's challenges and straight to a place of healing—practical steps that will take you from stressed to settled. No matter what you face, Rebekah proves that with God's grace, you can land in a place of resilience and joy.

SHANNON BREAM, #1 *New York Times* bestselling
author and anchor of *Fox News Sunday*

Rebekah Lyons is a one-of-a-kind woman who has compassion for all that we have in common. This book on resilience is incredibly important in the complex world we all share. While we live in a world of division, we share the same emotions, fears, and unavoidable periods of suffering. What we don't share is the capacity to deal with those debilitating aspects of our lives and ways to rise above those periods of chaos. This book is written for everyone, no matter what you are dealing with. I wish I had access to this book during my periods of unspeakable loss, cancer, and the failures that continue to haunt me with regret. There are paths through the storms, and Rebekah's faith, wisdom, and experience can help guide you through them.

SCOTT HAMILTON, cancer survivor, Olympic
gold medalist, and serial optimist

Rebekah Lyons has given us a tremendous gift in this resource! *Resilience* is a trustworthy guide through life's most challenging hardships. She uses her personal experiences to encourage readers to see the goodness of God in the hardest of times. After reading this, you will be on your way to a resilient life!

JONATHAN POKLUDA, pastor of Harris Creek Baptist Church, bestselling author, and host of the *Becoming Something* podcast

In a time when hopelessness is growing in the hearts of people around the world, Rebekah Lyons has developed an antidote and offered up a strategy for developing the resilience we need in order to endure and regain hope. This book will create grit that lasts for generations.

TONI COLLIER, speaker and author of *Brave Enough to Be Broken*

Building a Resilient Life is filled with Rebekah's powerful testimony and wisdom on how to practice courage and cling to God in a world that feels unsteady and heavy. I felt her humility and love on every page, like a friend wanting to impart her years of tear-soaked experiences with vulnerability and rawness. She doesn't promote a "put your head in the sand and pretend it's not there" approach to living, but quite the opposite. She urges us, as people practicing the way of Jesus, to press in to the hardest places—exposing our fears, pains, and anxieties and how they can teach us and drive us toward God.

HILLARY SCOTT TYRRELL, recording artist, wife, and mom

The last few years have been overwhelming for us all. No one has been left untouched. And many are struggling to move beyond the survival malaise and into the life that Jesus offers. In this deeply inspiring yet practical book, Rebekah Lyons shows, with compassion, skill, and love, how to build a life of resilience. I believe this is the book so many have been waiting for to take steps to cultivating a resilient heart.

JON TYSON, author and pastor (church.nyc)

ALSO BY REBEKAH LYONS

Freefall to Fly

You Are Free

Rhythms of Renewal

A Surrendered Yes

REBEKAH LYONS

BESTSELLING AUTHOR OF *RHYTHMS OF RENEWAL*

BUILDING A
RESILIENT
LIFE

HOW ADVERSITY AWAKENS
STRENGTH, HOPE, AND MEANING

ZONDERVAN
BOOKS

ZONDERVAN BOOKS

Building a Resilient Life
Copyright © 2023 by Rebekah Lyons

Requests for information should be addressed to:
Zondervan, *3900 Sparks Dr. SE, Grand Rapids, Michigan 49546*

Zondervan titles may be purchased in bulk for educational, business, fundraising, or sales
promotional use. For information, please email SpecialMarkets@Zondervan.com.

ISBN 978-0-310-36539-6 (hardcover)
ISBN 978-0-310-36715-4 (international trade paper edition)
ISBN 978-0-310-36542-6 (audio)
ISBN 978-0-310-36541-9 (ebook)

The author is represented by Meredith Brock at The Brock Agency.

Cover design: Riley Moody
Cover illustration: Hannah Joiner Crosby
Interior design: Aaron Campbell and Denise Froehlich

Printed in the United States of America

23 24 25 26 27 LBC 5 4 3 2 1

To Joy—
who is everything her name suggests
and who taught me
the gift of resilience

*Not only that, but we rejoice
in our sufferings, knowing that
suffering produces endurance,
and endurance produces character,
and character produces hope.*

ROMANS 5:3–4 ESV

CONTENTS

RULE FOUR: MAKE MEANING

RULE FIVE: ENDURE TOGETHER

INTRODUCTION

AN ERA OF OVERWHELM

CHAPTER ONE

AN ERA OF OVERWHELM

*Ambiguous loss makes us feel incompetent. It erodes our
sense of mastery and destroys our belief in the world as a
fair, orderly, and manageable place.*

DR. PAULINE BOSS

It was World Mental Health Day 2019. Gabe and I were minutes
away from taking the stage in front of eight thousand university
students in Virginia. Backstage, our eldest son, an eighteen-year-
old with Down syndrome, glimpsed a tall stack of giant chocolate
chip cookies covered under a glass cloche. Eyes locked in hot pursuit, he would not be denied. Cade lifted the glass and began to
scarf down cookies as quickly as possible, while we busied ourselves with details for the event. Within moments, Gabe noticed
Cade, armed with cookies in one hand, glass in the other, and tried
to carefully intervene. There was only one problem: Cade would
not give up his death grip on the glass.

What began as a cautious parenting redirection quickly escalated.

Crumbs and cookie bits flew into the air and onto the floor. Voices rose. Bodies tensed. Cade squeezed tight as Gabe tried to pull the lid from his hand. Too late. Cade jerked away and the glass broke into shards. In the chaos, I looked down to see Gabe's forearm covered in blood. Someone quickly arrived with a first aid kit to assist Gabe, while Cade stayed huddled on the floor, gripping a triangular piece of glass with three sharp edges, cortisol surging and body trembling. Fearful of more bloodshed in the stress and confusion, I knelt and spoke to Cade in calm tones. "Please give Mommy the glass."

He refused. I tried again, this time with a promise.

"If you give Mommy the glass, you can have one last cookie."

After thinking over his options for a minute, he slowly complied, then gulped down his fifth cookie, while my fourteen-year-old daughter looked on in disgust.

"How could you reward Cade after he hurt Dad?" she demanded in hot tears.

I tried to explain that sometimes negotiation is necessary when danger is present. She wasn't interested in nuance.

With Cade's arm bandaged, Gabe and I took a deep breath before stepping onstage. The ironies weren't lost on me. Our topic was "Establishing Rhythms to Sustain Mental Health," and there I was with my own anxiety working its way through me. What's more, we were addressing college students—a group our son Cade would never be included in given his own mental disability. This would be our last large event before COVID-19 lockdowns began. A moment of stubbornness and pandemonium backstage provided a glimpse of the future, a harbinger of things to come.

Cade's unspoken frustration grew. As the weeks went on, his undisclosed anxiety turned inward. He resisted every transition, whether getting in or out of the car, on or off the bus, in or out of restaurants, school, or church. Cade began to take this defiance out on himself, slamming his head into windows and walls at mealtime or into his headboard at bedtime. He slapped his face in anger or froze during family dinners while the rest of us tried to console him. He sat for an hour in the dark and refused to lie down after a lengthy tuck in, hitting his head against the headboard, which we could hear from our bedroom on the other side of the wall. My insomnia reached an all-time high as I whispered chronic prayers for rescue and peace.

Later that fall on a family trip home from Florida, Cade refused to get out of the rental car at the airport. Concerned we might miss our flight home, I ran around the parking garage in search of a wheelchair, finally finding one three parking sections away. When we tried to gently shift him into the wheelchair, Cade grabbed onto the car door handle with a death grip and shook violently, eyes locked in a silent scream. He wouldn't budge, and if we didn't leave soon, we wouldn't make it home. We reluctantly left Gabe and Cade behind and scrambled toward security, hoping to make it to our flight before they closed the gate.

On our way toward the concourse, we all cried and argued, living out a real-time trauma.

One child declared, "I hate Cade!" while another admonished, "You don't mean that!" In that moment, I knew our reality had shifted. Years of patience and restrained anger bubbled over, ruined by yet another uncontrollable circumstance. Fortunately, Cade relented, and while he and Gabe barely made the evening flight, the damage was done.

Our family would recover, but we would never be the same.

After we arrived home, we went through months of behavioral therapy and family counseling. We made multiple attempts to schedule an MRI for Cade, hoping to discover whether something had changed neurologically. Every doctor refused the exploratory procedure because Cade would have to be put under to lie still. Because he has Down syndrome, his airways are smaller than those of most typical kids his age, which creates a risk for asphyxiation under anesthesia. In addition, because Cade is nonverbal, he would have limited ability to alert us if anything went wrong. Each of these doctors refused to put him under for an exploratory procedure, telling us they'd only sedate Cade if it was completely necessary.

It was a dark season, and I never wrote about it online or spoke about it in public. I hid everything to protect Cade, but inside I was spiraling in grief. In many ways, I identified with Cade. As he spiraled, I spiraled, desperate to understand what he could not explain, desperate to comfort his fears and anxieties even as he was pushing me away.

Sometimes I glimpsed a momentary breakthrough when I knelt close, whispered, and waited. "Mommy loves Cade. Do you want a hug?" In those patient, quiet moments, Cade would eventually start bawling and let me hold him. I caught a glimpse of his non-verbal agony, deeper than his defiant exterior. *When he wept, I saw him fully.* I also saw the rest of us fully, breaking under the weight of change and loss, struggling with our limits to help him. Cade gifted us with honesty, no filter by which to pretend.

IT WAS A DARK SEASON, AND I NEVER WROTE ABOUT IT ONLINE OR SPOKE ABOUT IT IN PUBLIC. I HID EVERYTHING TO PROTECT CADE, BUT INSIDE I WAS SPIRALING IN GRIEF.

We were losing our son, and this was the kind of loss I'd never experienced. It was one thing to get a Down syndrome diagnosis at birth and experience the ambiguity that comes with an unknown childhood. Would Cade be able to talk, run, read, fall in love? After months of surrender in the first year of his life, we rallied and learned to live into a new normal, even though it was far different from anything we were prepared for.

Two decades later, this was a second loss. To know that Cade's engaging smile was fading—the one I'd grown to love and rarely saw anymore—felt too great to bear. It was a loss so gradual and extended I almost couldn't perceive it. Over time, it became the grief of a thousand tiny cuts, every interaction, every day, every eggshell we danced on to keep going.

One afternoon, I went for a walk in the woods. Cade had had another outburst days before, and the stress of that one, along with all the other outbursts, weighed heavily on our marriage. Gabe and

I argued constantly about how to best parent him, nerves frayed and on edge. Our teenagers were exhausted and began to avoid any attempt to spend time together as a family. We tried our best to shield Joy—our youngest daughter we adopted two years prior at the age of five, who also has Down syndrome—but she saw enough to know that Cade was sad.

I walked in silence in those woods, listening to the sound of crunching leaves underfoot, tears streaming down my cheeks. I finally spoke, begging God through tears, "Are you going to lift this?" I felt no end in sight, full of exhaustion and devoid of hope.

Within moments I heard in my spirit, *Not yet. But I'll be here for as many wailing walks as you need.*

This wasn't the answer I wanted. In my plan, God was supposed to bring rescue and relief. Wasn't he the one who makes our burden light? How long must we sustain this endless loop of grief? We were eighteen months into a new reality since the cookies and the broken glass, and I was languishing. I didn't want to keep walking this story out. All of my attempts had failed, and there I stood, pleading with God to sweep in and remove the pain. Little did I know that this would be the beginning of something new, a journey that would require complete trust and resilience. In the face of adversity, I would uncover strength, hope, and meaning.

Still, somehow the words were a comfort. I felt supported knowing that the presence of God wouldn't leave in the middle of my defeat. I remembered a promise given to Joshua before he pressed on in the seemingly insurmountable task of taking possession of the promised land: "The LORD himself goes before you and will be with you; he will never leave you nor forsake you. Do not be afraid; do not be discouraged" (Deuteronomy 31:8). The assurance that God would be with me through all of this, no matter how difficult the circumstance—just as he had been with Joshua—gave me a sense of God's presence and peace.

With renewed strength we visited our family counselor, who helped us understand each shift in Cade's life in the past two years. We'd moved. He'd switched schools. We'd brought his new little sister, Joy, home from China. Cade had always been one to go and be with friends. He had structure that helped him thrive, even in the middle of so much change, until the pandemic hit.

After much learning and discovery, we decided to try medication meant to help balance out his severe mood swings. Within three days, balance came. That night, he was goofing off at bedtime, just as he had in years past. I turned to Gabe and said, "We just saw a glimpse of our son."

Still, we didn't want to get our hopes up. After all, the doctors told us it would be a month before we would know if the medication was helping. It did help, but there were side effects. He lost ten pounds in eight weeks on an already slender frame. He struggled with bladder control and had accidents at home and at school. We kept adjusting.

I'd love to say we've figured it out, but we're still walking the road. Some days are easier, and some days are harder. Still, this glimpse of hope gave us the courage to keep going, even in the face of so much tangible and ambiguous loss.

Ambiguous Loss: The New Reality

We're all familiar with loss. We've lost jobs, loved ones, beloved pets, homes, communities. These losses leave a void in our lives, one that's easy to pinpoint. When these things happen, we can adopt certain healing techniques to help us overcome grief and move into a more resilient way of existence. What about when these losses are more covert, more ambiguous? How do we overcome the grief we can't seem to name?

Dr. Pauline Boss, an educator and researcher, coined the clinical term "ambiguous loss" in the 1970s to describe a relational disorder characterized by a lack of clarity surrounding the physical *or* psychological loss of a loved one.

Type One ambiguous loss occurs when there is *physical absence with psychological presence*. The death of a loved one, the divorce of our spouse, the moving away of a child, or the giving up of a child for adoption can summon feelings we don't know how to process. These unwanted circumstances in life leave us with unresolved pain.

Type Two occurs when there is *psychological absence with physical presence*. Due to addiction, depression, Alzheimer's disease, or other chronic mental or physical illnesses, a loved one may be emotionally or cognitively gone or missing, but they are still physically in our lives. This leaves us going through the motions of love while still feeling alone.[1]

When we suffer ambiguous loss, there's no sense of resolution or closure. Doesn't this describe so many other forms of loss? It's the loss we feel when our expectations don't quite work out or when people walk away. It's the loss of a dream, a sense of purpose, or our security when finances unexpectedly shift. As I studied this type of loss, it resonated deeply with my experience. Ambiguous loss— wasn't this what I was going through with Cade? I'd lost a part of my son, a part I couldn't quite identify, a way of relating to him I once considered "normal."

This type of illogical, chaotic grief can last for months or decades, a sporadic sadness that may surface during certain moments of life. As I studied the concept, I realized it didn't mean something was wrong with me. It is perfectly natural and expected that a caregiver will grieve losses that occur along the way without full resolution. The problem was that I felt anger in the grief, anger that I wasn't strong or positive enough or that I wasn't able to bounce back. Looking back, I felt shame that I wasn't all that resilient.

Naming What We've Lost

Like me, like Cade, so many of us are dealing with some form of ambiguous loss. Haven't we all felt out of control, at a loss, grasping for any form of familiarity or structure, even if we can't exactly name the loss? If we're being honest, we're left with a sense of being overwhelmed.

I wonder what you, dear reader, have lost. Maybe it feels ambiguous, especially in your current situation. What if you took the time to name it? What ways of living, what schedules, what routines, or what disrupted career plans and dreams are you grieving without resolution? Perhaps it's a marriage that is drifting apart and you can't quite put your finger on why it's happening, or a child who has rejected you or God or both. Maybe it's not a child with special needs who's prone to outbursts; maybe *you're* the one with outbursts.

Maybe you can look back and see an era when you were flourishing, but now you feel like you're caught in an eddy of grief. Perhaps you once felt strong, but now you feel weaker than ever. Or you feel bent to the point of breaking and you're not sure if you'll ever bounce back. As we'll discuss in the coming chapters, it's that determination *to keep going*—whether in the face of ambiguous loss, chaos, or turmoil—that we call "resilience." It seems we need to develop resilience now more than ever.

Throughout the season of struggles with Cade, Gabe and I realized our resilience was being tested. Without practices to strengthen and fortify our resilience, particularly in such an ambiguous year of confusion, we wouldn't have the strength to help him flourish again. So I set out to understand what it meant to cultivate a life of resilience in a chaotic, turbulent, ever-changing world.

A New Era Calls for a New Resilience

Examine your own life. You still have the usual challenges—the piles of laundry on the couch, the school assignments left undone, the text from a friend who lost her job. You have a whole host of new challenges too—navigating complex and shaming social media messages, dealing with a political landscape that often reminds us that the sky is falling, wars and rumors of wars springing up overseas. This is just a partial list of the complexities we're dealing with as you read this book.

In the wake of all this adversity, we do our best to survive, but right about the time we feel we have our footing, the landscape seems to change. Remember when we only needed two weeks of quarantine to flatten the curve? We rallied at home and embraced cooking and sweatpants and TikTok dances. The needs kept changing over the subsequent two years, reducing our window of tolerance and resilience.

While mental health has historically grown *stronger* during wartime and crises in centuries past, these lockdowns were different.[2] Our mental health became *weaker*. With no clear enemy to fight and a constant confusion over how to rally and help our neighbors, combined with ongoing isolation, we began to feel that we had lost our agency. We began to feel helpless with no sense of meaning. This destructive combination heightened a pent-up need for control. The result? Some mental health professionals believe we are in one of the angriest and most anxious, depressed, and isolated eras of human history.

Instead of dealing with the pressures of life in healthy ways, we turn to coping mechanisms to numb ourselves to the stress and pain of this reality. Some turn to alcohol or pills, while others turn to work, entertainment, social media, or shopping. Recognizing the trend, the United States Centers for Disease Control and Prevention observed that "COVID-19 has had a major effect on our lives. Many of us are facing challenges that can be stressful and overwhelming. Learning to cope with stress in a healthy way will help you, the people you care about, and those around you become more resilient."[3]

Resilient? Is this even possible? If so, how do we pursue it?

In these pages, we'll engage the stories of people of resilience. We'll lean in and learn from research by experts in human behavior. Finally, we'll be grounded by the lasting truth of the Scriptures. My hope is that you'll come to understand how certain practices or rules can help you live a more resilient life.

What are those rules?

Rule 1: Name the Pain: Be Honest

Rule 2: Shift the Narrative: Renew Your Mind

Rule 3: Embrace Adversity: Train with Resistance

Rule 4: Make Meaning: Cultivate Beauty

Rule 5: Endure Together: Invite Others In

Applying those rules, we'll learn how to forge resilient lives, ones that withstand the most difficult moments of adversity. Together, we'll learn how to create resilient communities, tethered to withstand the pressures the world throws at us.

If you're experiencing adversity and wondering how long you can persevere, keep reading. Invite others into the journey too. Together, let's build lives that can thrive, no matter what form of adversity comes our way.

REFLECTIONS ON RESILIENCE

1. Have you taken the time to name the things you've lost over the last few years? If not, set aside thirty minutes to put together a list of what's different in your life.

2. Next to each item, summarize how it makes you feel. Use feeling words such as *angry*, *sad*, *lonely*, or *afraid*. Any feeling word will do.

3. Looking at your list of losses and your list of feelings, are you struggling to bounce back from a sense of ambiguous loss?

WHAT IS RESILIENCE, REALLY?

WHAT IS RESILIENCE, REALLY?

Do not judge me by my successes, judge me by how many times I fell down and got back up again.

NELSON MANDELA

When we moved away from New York City eight years ago, I harbored a secret longing that we'd return nine years later. All three kids would have graduated from high school, entered college, or started jobs. We would be free to return to the place where God got loud and I found my voice.

This longing ebbed and flowed during the subsequent years in the Tennessee South. It was quelled by the kindness of strangers and the beauty of rolling hills and then heightened when the charm and comforts lulled me to apathy and lostness of heart. I'd drift between the extremes of coming alive and drowning. I couldn't find my footing in the river between the banks of chaos and control.

What made New York City so beautiful, even when it was so

difficult? The surprise around every corner, the diversity in a million ways, the unexpected beauty in the middle of the muck. Most of all, it was the action. A life lived fully was not a theory in the city; it was a practice. And you had no option but to go out and begin again each day.

This daily practice of living life fully taught me many things. I learned to jump off a subway just before an addict got violent and to absorb and deflect a stranger screaming in my face while I held my daughter's hand. I learned to fight the elements in eleven-degree temps with the proper coat and wear knee-high rubber boots amid torrential spring rains or twenty-inch snow dumps in winter. I also learned how to carry a whimpering puppy with a broken leg on Christmas Eve until I found a vet's office that was open. I learned to survive when I was out of my element.

The learning wasn't just for me. Gabe learned how to kill sixty-two mice in our first two years. He learned that "No Standing Zone" meant "Don't leave your car for a second on this curb." He learned to recover said car from the towing lot twelve hundred dollars later.

Kennedy learned to let the ambulance medic cut off her brand-new bloodied winter coat when the tip of her pinky finger was sliced off while ice-skating in Central Park. Pierce learned how to respond to kids who called Cade stupid and retarded. Cade learned to fight for air during a croup attack at three in the morning while we waited on our street corner for a taxi to the hospital.

We also learned how to curate peace, joy, community, and beauty. I learned to sneak into a cathedral in the middle of a Tuesday to whisper a prayer for strength and love. To make every beautiful day a "picnic blanket on the lawn and tree climbing" day. To walk to church and invite friends over for lunch right after that. To discover a flower cart for only five dollars a bunch and adorn our dining table with peonies, tulips, roses, lilies, and gerbera daisies year-round.

Pierce memorized the heights of the tallest towers and where all the best trees to climb were located. In third grade he learned to busk for tips while playing his guitar in Central Park. Kennedy learned to walk her puppies for their favorite treats and take Cade's hand to keep him moving when he grew tired. Cade learned to climb boulders in Heckscher Playground and wait patiently by the glass at Central Park Zoo until the polar bears swam by to say hello.

New York is the place we found our resilience, both individually and collectively. When you've fought to love something—even a particular place—it's that love that pushes you to persevere and endure in the hardest of times. When you do, you find that the reward is joy, contentment, and gratitude. Not only for then, but also for now. Once you discover a grit that leads to growth or a passion that helps you persist, it's quite difficult to return to a life of ease.

In New York, we never had to manufacture adversity; it was a way of life. As they say, if you can make it here, you can make it anywhere. Looking back, I left that city stronger and more hopeful, with an overflowing abundance of meaning. Eight years later, with the onset of so much turmoil, I'm finding that the ease of comfort and the distraction of technology have robbed me of some of that. Thus I'm writing this book as much for me as for you. I'm asking these questions: *How do we cultivate a life that is meaningful when culture tempts us with the opposite? Why would we place ourselves in the face of adversity when our devices try to lull us to sleep?* I'm haunted that cultural critic Neil Postman was prophetic in his prediction nearly forty years ago in which he cited the view of Aldous Huxley, the author of *Brave New World*: "People will come to adore the technologies that undo their capacities to think."[1]

What Is Resilience?

There's no doubt in my mind that adversity cultivates resilience. Before we get ahead of ourselves, what does that really mean? Some psychologists define resilience as "the process of adapting well in the face of adversity, trauma, tragedy, threats, or significant sources of stress."[2]

The word *resilience* derives from the Latin term *resilire*, which means "to recoil or rebound," and made its debut in the English language in 1627. The first entry in the *Oxford English Dictionary* memorializes this as "an act of rebounding or springing back; rebound, recoil." The second definition of resilience was added in 1824, associated with elasticity: the "power of resuming an original shape or position after compression, bending, etc."

Popular culture seems to have limited the definition of resilience, using it to describe people who "bounce back." While I appreciate the sentiment, I see the term as being a bit broader. Bouncing back implies that resilience is something simple and quick, such as the return of a ball bounced against a wall time and time again. That we could simply be tossed and retrieved without eventually becoming cracked and deflated—wouldn't that be nice if it were true?

We are not people who simply bounce back. We experience all kinds of trouble. We endure unspeakable tragedy and ambiguous loss, both of which can take a lifetime to heal. We develop wounds and scars. Resilient people experience this pain with honesty and bravery, and they become stronger not despite the resistance but *because* of the resistance.

I might define resilience this way: our daily, consecrated act of remembering there is something far greater than our present troubles, which offers us the power to endure and emerge. In adversity, what is the *something greater* we are supposed to remember? In the gospel of John, the beloved apostle captures the promise of Jesus: "In this world you will have trouble. But take heart! I have overcome the world" (John 16:33).

See?

Jesus didn't promise us an easy existence. He didn't promise health, wealth, or prosperity in a world full of trite clichés and memes. He promised trouble. Hardship. Difficulty. He gave a further promise to overcome all hardship and difficulty on our behalf. He has overcome the world. With him, we can overcome too. This is holy resilience.

Healing begins the moment we speak what is true. The truth is, no matter the adversity we find ourselves in, we have access to a source of overcoming love that bears all things, believes all things, hopes all things, and endures all things (1 Corinthians 13:7 ESV). We may not *bounce* back in adversity, but we do find our legs to stand up again, powered by a love that never fails. That's resilience.

This ability to stand back up reminds me of the *Oxford English Dictionary*'s second definition of resilience: the "power of resuming an original shape or position after compression, bending, etc." There isn't a time limit for the compression, the bending, the absorbing of the aftershocks of pain or loss. Though we may resume our original shape—we look like some version of who we were before the adversity—there's something new about us. We have a new quality, a new strength.

As a mother who in her twenties gave birth to a son with severe cognitive challenges, in her thirties endured the sudden onset of panic, and in her forties lost a father after decades of mental struggle, I'm still learning what it means to bend under the weight of tumultuous seasons that feel accented by loss. This doesn't mean I haven't experienced significant joys along this exact same journey, for *pain always becomes purpose if you let it*. I'm simply acknowledging the narrative arc of my life in order to remember the original shape or position God intends for each of us, no matter the recurring adversity we find ourselves in.

PAIN ALWAYS BECOMES PURPOSE IF YOU LET IT.

What I'm struck by is that I haven't gone back to the original shape of who I was as a child—that would be regression. While I still look like Rebekah, there are scars from three Cesarean sections that brought Cade, Pierce, and Kennedy into the world. There are new wrinkles and laugh lines from saying yes to adopting Joy in our mid-forties. While I return to something that looks like me, I also become incrementally stronger, able to endure a little bit more. This endurance brings an inner quality that is renewed "day by day" (2 Corinthians 4:16). This is true resilience.

If more than four decades of living have taught me anything, it's that the ones who "bounce back" may not be the most resilient. The people who've weathered storms throughout the entirety of their lives, who've stayed when it would have been easier to leave, who've lived with integrity and commitment, who've both resumed their original shape and undergone internal transformation? These are the resilient ones.

Let's go a step further. Let's talk about what resilience isn't.

What Resilience Is Not

I hear the word *resilience* and conjure up images of a person who is the epitome of pure strength. No circumstance can sway them. No ill word or unplanned encounter gets in their way. They stand strong, no matter the cost. Often their confidence makes them appear to be unbreakable. Does this make a person resilient?

Consider Aesop's fable, in which a mighty oak tree asked a reed, "Why do you not plant your feet deeply in the ground, and raise your head boldly in the air as I do?" The reed responded, "I am contented with my lot. I may not be so grand, but I think I am safer." The tree scoffed and said, "Safe! Who shall pluck me up by the roots or bow my head to the ground?" That same day, a hurricane swept through, tearing the mighty tree up by its roots and casting it uselessly to the ground, while the little reed, though bending to the force of the wind, never lost its footing. When the storm passed, the reed soon stood upright again, stretching tall.[3]

Resilience isn't unyielding willpower that pushes through any obstacle or withstands any force. Resilience allows us to be flexible and adaptable. We bend but aren't broken; we are wounded but learn how to heal. This is the picture of resilience we can learn how to cultivate.

Resilience isn't about sheer strength, and it's not about stubborn persistence either. Resilience is faithful perseverance. There is a subtle and distinct difference. Persistence is a single-mindedness no matter the obstacle—a trait that can be harmful in toxic circumstances or when your stated goal is unattainable. Perseverance, on the other hand, is a steady determination to choose to grow and learn from obstacles or difficult situations, some of which can last a lifetime. Resilience not only bends but also receives permission to bow out before it breaks. Resilience knows when it's time to stop. There are some storms we must bend low to endure; there are others we run from as fast as we can. A resilient mind knows the difference.

Resilience is not naive optimism either. Resilience is contentment in the acceptance of *what is*. The apostle Paul, who suffered persecution, stoning, shipwrecks, and snake bites, is a picture of resilience. Time and time again, he suffered, and time and time again, he found the grace to endure. What was the key to his resilience? He learned the *secret* to being content. As he wrote to the church in Philippi, "I know how to make do with little, and I know how to make do with a lot. In any and all circumstances I have learned the secret of being content—whether well fed or hungry, whether in abundance or in need. I am able to do all things through him who strengthens me" (Philippians 4:12–13 CSB). This popular passage is often taken out of context. These verses are not about achievement, but rather about contentment in all circumstances. Resilience is the ability to be content, to accept what is, and to have the courage to surrender to Christ anything that comes our way.

Resilience in Unchangeable Circumstances

Reinhold Niebuhr wrote the prayer now known as the "Serenity Prayer." In its original form, the prayer read, "Father, give us courage to change what must be altered, serenity to accept what cannot be helped, and the insight to know the one from the other." He later rewrote and reordered it, "God, grant me the serenity to accept the things I cannot change, courage to change the things I can, and wisdom to know the difference."[4]

Niebuhr understood a deep truth about resilience. We all encounter circumstances that we know must change, and we should wield everything in our power to change those things. There are times, though, when the change we desire simply doesn't happen. There are times, too, when the change we want is little more than a pipe dream or it's not what God knows is best. In those situations, we bend low to whisper the prayer of Jesus in Gethsemane: "Not my will, but yours be done" (Luke 22:42).

Over the past few years, we've all endured a great deal of change. So much of what we've dreamed for our lives has morphed, shifted, or even evaporated. In this era of unending change, we can sit with the Serenity Prayer, meditate on it, and learn the resilient peace of saying, "Not my will, Lord, but yours be done."

We can also turn to other prayers. Over these past years, the liturgy that ministered more to my heart than any other is Douglas McKelvey's "For the Death of a Dream." It was this liturgy that spoke to me in the wee hours of the morning when I'd wake up with sadness or anxiety. I'd crawl out of my bed quietly, arrange a soft pallet on my closet floor, and open the Scriptures, my journal, and a book of prayers. The first night I stumbled across these words, I began to weep, having no idea I was holding on to such grief:

O Christ, in whom the final fulfillment of all hope is held and secure, I bring to you now the weathered fragments of my former dreams, the broken pieces of my expectations, the rent patches of hopes worn thin, the shards of some shattered image of life as I once thought it would be. What I so wanted has not come to pass . . . and in my head, I know that you are sovereign even over this—over my tears, my confusion, and my disappointment. *But I still feel, in this moment, as if I have been abandoned, as if you do not care that these hopes have collapsed to rubble.*

And yet I know this is not so. You are the sovereign of my sorrow. You apprehend a wider sweep with wiser eyes than mine. My history bears the fingerprints of grace. You were always faithful, though I could not always trace quick evidence of your presence in my pain, yet did you remain at work. . . .

So let me remain tender now, to how you would teach me. My disappointments reveal so much about my own agenda for my life, and the ways I quietly demand that it should play out: free of conflict, free of pain, free of want.

My dreams are all so small. . . .

Now take this dream, this chaff of my desire, and give it back reformed and remade according to your better vision, or do not give it back at all. Here in the ruins of my wrecked expectation, let me make this best confession: Not my dreams, O Lord, not my dreams, but yours, be done. Amen.[5]

Isn't this the whole of the Christian life? Pain that ebbs and flows, joy that ebbs and flows—two extremes that coexist and keep us broken and whole at the same time? Life is less about mastery and more about the unfolding of faith in the process of being made new.

It's this liturgy that encapsulates the Christian's bent toward resilience. We are truly resilient when we bring ourselves to Christ, weathered and worn, and allow ourselves to be filled and remade in the original shape of our Creator. When we acknowledge that our lives do not look like we planned or imagined, we begin to make our peace with this truth. As we embrace that peace, we're beginning to be remade in the image of Christ.

The "Now and Not Yet" Character of Resilience

I wish building resilience was a one-and-done thing, that we need only to die to our dreams once, surrender, and then pick up and move on. But the character of resilience is something altogether different. It's about *becoming* people of resilience. This becoming takes time and practice. We will experience multiple storms over the course of our lives, some short and some with no end date in sight. Each of these storms will teach us a little more about resilience if only we let it.

A life of resilience is one that weathers storms. It's a life that is humble, surrendered, able to imagine new dreams when old dreams die. It's a life that remembers God's promise to be with us, even to the end of the age. It's a life that believes that Jesus has truly overcome the world.

This means as we learn resilience, we hold the tension in the now and the not yet. Even as we experience the chill of winter, we know the warmth of summer is coming. When circumstances feel dark and looming, we expect the sun to rise at dawn. We know that though some seasons are fallow, others will yield an abundant harvest that is visible to all.

As you read this book, try to hold the tension between the now and not yet. Understand that though you may have trouble now, Christ *in you* has overcome the world. In the now and not yet, you'll begin to discover something about resilience—what's more important than overcoming something is knowing how to endure it with the help of our mighty God who overcomes. You'll grasp how to be bent low without being broken. You'll comprehend how to be raised to something that looks like new life. This is resilience.

Where should we begin our deeper exploration of resilience? We begin at that acute point where some give up while others do not. We start at the point of pain.

REFLECTIONS ON RESILIENCE

1. Can you point to any seasons of adversity in your life that made you stronger? What practices helped you navigate those times?

2. List the seasons of adversity that seem to have no end date. For each, identify which challenges you can walk away from and which you must endure.

3. Write a note to yourself—one that encourages you to endure in your present struggles. After writing it, how do you feel?

THE PAIN OF ADVERSITY

THE PAIN OF ADVERSITY

Character cannot be developed in ease and quiet. Only through experience of trial and suffering can the soul be strengthened, vision cleared, ambition inspired, and success achieved.

HELEN KELLER

In 2018, Gabe and I felt the distinct impression that our family wasn't complete. We were in our mid-forties, quickly approaching a time when the kids would be out of the house. Still, there was a nagging feeling. Were we supposed to adopt? The whisper of God is much like sand in your shoe. You can't shake it, and it can become quite irritating if you ignore it, no matter how long or how hard you try.

If you've read *Rhythms of Renewal*, you know the full story, but suffice it to say that God interrupted our lives with the option to *choose* Down syndrome this time around when a dear friend, Meredith, texted us a photo of a girl on the other side of the world. As details quickly fell into place, we knew that God had prepared us seventeen years earlier when we became parents of Cade, and it was time to trust him again. So we began to plan and prepare for our Down syndrome bookends, thirteen years apart. Instead of empty nesting in three years, we were going back to kindergarten, thus beginning our journey with Joy.

Joy was abandoned at a police station in China at four months of age. While we don't have specific details on Joy's family of origin, in Chinese culture, the very act of leaving a baby with the authorities would have been considered an act of compassion and a desperate cry for help. Often, families of newborns with special needs that lack the resources or social support to care for their babies place their child in the hands of rescue workers, where they receive immediate care. That's exactly how Joy found her way into a Chinese orphanage just four months into life.

This particular orphanage was in a rural part of the Guangdong province—a smaller orphanage than those located near large cities—and came with a distinct advantage. Just as a child in a smaller school may receive more individualized attention, children in smaller Chinese orphanages may receive some level of consistent care and interaction with the other children in their community. This type of care and community can offer a less fractured sense of connection and belonging.

Four years into her time at this orphanage, Joy was sent on a train through the night all the way to Beijing to a foster home affectionately called the "Little House of Brave," which typically houses eight to ten children awaiting heart surgery, cared for by several faithful nannies.

Joy didn't happen to need heart surgery, but God knew she needed to be on that train. This is when we discovered her and were grateful to be granted approval by China to adopt her. We even had the privilege to meet and talk to her via FaceTime. We were sent videos and pictures of Joy attending music and dance classes, learning how to cook, and celebrating every milestone with her best friends. She keeps in touch with them to this day because those friends were adopted by other families in Nashville.

But then something changed.

Before we were granted permission to travel to China to finalize the adoption, the government sent Joy *back* to her original orphanage ten months after arriving at Little House of Brave. To this day, I can't fathom what it meant for this five-year-old girl's heart to have to leave Little House of Brave after ten months of bonding, only to be returned to the orphanage she'd previously left. Her entire world had changed in those ten short months. She had made something like a *family*.

Even worse for us, on that fateful day in May, communication with Joy was completely cut off. Gabe and I were determined to get to China as fast as we possibly could. We prayed and put out the call to our community to pray for doors to fly open, to accelerate our travel date. Though it didn't happen as quickly as we would have liked, months later, we boarded a plane the week after Thanksgiving.

Upon arriving, we made plans to finalize the adoption. Joy rode two hours to the government office where we would meet her and sign the official documents. She arrived dressed to the nines in a layered dress with gold embroidery on her collar, tights and pink shoes, bows in her braided hair. At five years old, she was also wearing a diaper and had taken a bottle twice the day before in her orphanage bedroom that housed eighteen cribs. This was her understanding of home.

Joy glanced at me from a distance and clutched the woman who held her. They followed us into a room where her caregiver peeled her off her body and forced her into my arms before shutting the door and leaving the room. The rest of what happened is hazy. Somehow Joy ran for the door, and somehow I was crawling after her. She clung to her water-filled bottle, so we kept refilling it to comfort her as silent tears streamed down her cheeks.

She fought me hard, resisting and pushing, but I held her until she finally wore out. To her, we were yet another transition to a new unknown. She wanted to go back to what she knew—the room with eighteen cribs—because that felt safer. She had no framework for a forever family, no concept of a secure and consistent home.

My heart broke open as I held her. How many times had God tried to convince me he was a good Father? How many times had I fought against him, wanting to remain "orphaned," feeling safer in my shame? God could call me daughter, but it would take his Spirit to help me trust enough to call him "*Abba*, Father" back (see Romans 8:14–17). This would be the situation for Joy as well. We could call her daughter once the paperwork was signed, but it would take days, weeks, even months before she truly understood we weren't going to leave her.

To our utter shock and amazement, Joy began to show tiny

glimpses of trust by sundown that evening. She offered a shy grin when she met her big sister, Kennedy, on FaceTime, who spoke to her in Mandarin for the first time. She met her two big brothers and showed them the toy "baby" we'd given her that afternoon. When we tucked her under her new blanket in the hotel's pack 'n play, she grinned up from her bedtime bottle as we sang "Twinkle, Twinkle, Little Star" and "Jesus Loves Me" while stroking her hair.

Joy had been in and out of different facilities and homes, moving here and there, and while we had no idea how many people had been responsible for her care, she was with us now. She had found her forever family for the first time, and we would learn together from there.

Within three days, Joy potty trained herself just by being given the opportunity. By the fifth day of being with us, she dropped formula and ate everything we offered her. As she grew more comfortable with us, her curiosity and laughter came out, as if both had been hidden below the surface.

As wonderful as it all was, the first year at home still presented challenges. Joy had night terrors almost every other night, and a cautious, untrusting look crossed her face every time we left the room. I learned to be present as her body physically grieved what she might never have the words to express.

Joy has been with us four years now, and her night terrors have slowly faded. It has taken some time, with relapses along the way, but she has adapted to our family and life in the States. She plays with friends, attends school, and loves church. She embraces new challenges, and though she couldn't say it quite this way, she allows each of those experiences to change her. Joy is our family's living, breathing example of resilience. Her story has allowed me to take a hard look at the way adversity affects each of us and how we can either break under the weight of adversity or bend and become more resilient.

Adversity Awakens Resilience

I don't know anyone who has been through as much adversity as Joy. She was born with Down Syndrome in a country that doesn't deal well with difference. She was dropped off on the doorstep of a police station. She was moved from orphanage to orphanage. Though we know we made the right decision, her adoption into our family meant she had to learn a new country and language. She has shown incredible resilience in the few short years she's been with our family.

I've found myself challenged by Joy, asking God to put a little of her resilience into my own life. Joy reminds me of the apostle Paul's teaching about the power of the gospel living in us:

> But we have [the gospel of Jesus] in jars of clay to show that this all-surpassing power is from God and not from us. We are hard pressed on every side, but not crushed; perplexed, but not in despair; persecuted, but not abandoned; struck down, but not destroyed. We always carry around in our body the death of Jesus, so that the life of Jesus may also be revealed in our body. For we who are alive are always being given over to death for Jesus' sake, so that his life may also be revealed in our mortal body. So then, death is at work in us, but life is at work in you. . . .

Therefore we do not lose heart. Though outwardly we are wasting away, yet inwardly we are being renewed day by day. For our light and momentary troubles are achieving for us an eternal glory that far outweighs them all. So we fix our eyes not on what is seen, but on what is unseen, since what is seen is temporary, but what is unseen is eternal. (2 Corinthians 4:7–12, 16–18)

Since bringing Joy home, I've contemplated these words, trying to understand what they meant for me in my own quest to cultivate resilience in the midst of chaos. I discovered the Bible doesn't promise we'll have an easy, carefree life. In fact, it teaches quite the opposite. We will be hard pressed, perplexed, and struck down. In other words, we will experience significant adversity. Still, Paul promised that if we face adversity head-on with the power of the gospel and practice inner renewal day by day, we can cultivate a life of resilience.

We Have a Choice

I wonder what kind of adversity you've been through. Maybe the loss of a job, a loved one, a marriage. Starting a job, raising a child, committing to marriage. Realizing you don't have enough money to pay the bills. Discovering you can't bear children, or the child you bore has a life-threatening addiction. A parent with a disease that requires significant medical attention. Maybe you're the parent.

Adversity is a fact of life. It comes to all of us, whether in the form of personal problems or collective, community issues. As believers in Christ, we're bound to suffer even more adversity as we live countercultural lives in a world antagonistic to faith. No one loves adversity. That's why our bodies freak out, our anxiety spikes in difficult times, our tempers shorten, and we reach for coping mechanisms.

There are two kinds of adversity: the kind we can't control, the adversity that is unexpected, such as a health scare, a marriage upended, a child in crisis—which is what Joy has endured her entire life—and the kind we take on voluntarily, such as growing a family, shifting careers, or moving across the country. Whether we initiate adversity or it happens when we least expect it, both require us to pause and pay attention to the way it impacts us.

When we're in the middle of adversity, survival is a struggle. We still have work, family, and community obligations to maintain. When prolonged adversity is layered with ongoing responsibilities, feelings of overwhelm, defeat, or anxiety can creep in. If we allow those feelings to take hold and don't push through them into resilience, we'll find ourselves heading toward discouragement and despair.

While we may feel anxious or defeated, these feelings indicate that we're veering off track and something needs to shift. We invite God into our struggle and share our overwhelm, asking him to reveal what he wants to gift us in this season. Trials offer us the gift of maturity and growth. They uncover what we'd rather avoid and nudge us toward healing and resilience.

———————————

TRIALS OFFER US THE GIFT OF MATURITY AND GROWTH.

———————————

Since we live in an age of adversity, we are met with a choice. We can give up, which leads to defeat and despair, or we can stay connected to God, ourselves, and one another and move toward resilience. Adversity awakens us to what will ultimately guide us toward a more resilient life.

A Practitioner's Manual

If I've learned anything from Joy, it's that when we endure adversity with positivity, curiosity, and reliance on God and community, we build lives of resilience. In my experience and research, I've identified five rules, mentioned in chapter 1, and a few practices that go along with them. These rules allow us to develop resilience in our everyday lives. There may be more, but the techniques of resilience development in this book have been tried-and-true for me and the people in my life. Use this book as a practitioner's manual. Examine each resilience-building technique in the upcoming chapters and ask, *How can I apply these techniques in my life when I'm confronted with adversity?* Then commit to regularly practice building resilience.

Adversity will try to take you out if you let it. If you allow curiosity, love, and laughter to lead you in and through adversity—just as Joy did—you'll emerge a more resilient person. Let's engage these practices of resilience together.

REFLECTIONS ON RESILIENCE

1. List the current adversities in your life. Which ones have you taken on voluntarily? Which ones were unexpected?

2. Make a list of the most resilient people you know. What characteristics do they share in common?

3. As you walk through this book, think of someone you can invite along on this journey of resilience. Commit to invite them into the process.

RULE ONE

NAME THE PAIN

BE HONEST

When I think about what thwarts our resilience, particularly as it relates to our physical, mental, and spiritual health, I believe the barrier to resilience is pain. Cancer ravages the body and makes it less resilient; anxiety plagues our mental health and leaves us unable to tend to everyday tasks; doubt keeps us locked in our shame and disconnects us from God.

If we're going to pursue resilience and withstand the chaos of the world, we begin by acknowledging when we feel pain. How do we identify and name it? We cannot heal what is hidden. We must begin with the question, *Where does it hurt?*

My friend Seth Haines wrote, "Pain is the divine proclamation, the thunderous wakeup call. It shouts to us, 'Something is broken!' If we wake to the call, pain directs us to a proper hope."[1] Seth is right. Pain points us to the place of our brokenness, the places we lack resilience. So if we're going to get serious about building resilience, we must name the pain.

In this section, we'll discover how to recognize our sin and shame, confess it to others, and invite others into our pain so we can find healing. We'll see how this healing sets the stage for further resilience training.

This section won't be easy, but I promise it'll be worth it. And it only gets better from here. Grab your journal and a pen. Take a deep breath. Together let's wade into the pain.

THE WEIGHT
OF SHAME

THE WEIGHT OF SHAME

Certainly nobody of us is spared suffering at one time or another, but everybody in the midst of suffering is given a chance to bear testimony of the human potential at its best. Which is to turn a personal tragedy into a human triumph.

VIKTOR FRANKL

One month into quarantine, I found a pattern developing at home. It took a moment for our family to realize that seemingly endless spans of time with those you love *without a plan* is not the easiest thing in the world. We needed something to *do*, to focus on. So we lived out different expectations in this season.

Gabe treated the pandemic as an ongoing research project, with countless hours spent researching and mobilizing friends in our community for whatever the future might hold. The kids stayed "busy" 24-7—snacking, completing school assignments, playing outdoors, streaming shows, more snacking—which meant the dishes, clothes, and garbage piled up. With everyone in one place for what felt like infinity, I took on the role of "domestic chaos manager" like it was my full-time job! As you can imagine, the pressure mounted.

I didn't have a place of escape or a release valve, so I obsessed about whatever I could control. I developed a sort of domestic hyper-vigilance, devoted to cleaning out the fridge, organizing closets, and rearranging the pantry, garage, and basement. Though these tasks took quite some time, once I got into it, I found other things that needed my attention—color-coding bookshelves, sorting junk and dresser drawers, emptying the attic. I didn't stop until every tiny thing had its place. When I thought I was finished, I wasn't. With six hungry (and sometimes bored) humans, there was always a fresh stack of dirty dishes in the sink or a damp pile of towels in front of the washing machine. And so I'd commence the cycle again.

My life became an exercise in chronic cleaning and purging, with an obsessive need for outer order. Why? Maybe I thought it would create inner order. Perhaps I needed a sense of control in an otherwise uncontrollable world. Whatever the reason, I felt some sense of a euphoric high seeing a pile of trash hauled away to the dump, bins of clothes dropped off at a donation center, or a freshly cleaned-out fridge. While decluttering and organization are essential for creativity and workflow in a healthy seasonal rhythm, I took it a step further. Daily maintenance became my highest priority, a laser-focused coping mechanism that helped me *feel* better because things *looked* better.

This compulsion spilled into my relationship with Gabe and the kids. Organizing took precedence over presence, play, and rest. I grew agitated when they were sitting around because I never sat down, and my voice seemed to rise in frustration with them before I noticed it was happening. All this work, so little sleep—it lit every nerve on fire. I overreacted to the simplest disagreement, emotions spiraling out of control. It became evident to all—including myself—that I was *losing* it.

Gabe and I had always been on the same page, particularly when it came to instructing our children, but he began to confront me both privately and when they were around. On any given afternoon, I found myself in my closet—blaming myself, dejected about losing control.

I'm a terrible mother.

A terrible wife.

I will never get this right.

I make everything worse.

I heard these voices daily in my head and felt alone in my shame. Would the house (and the people in it) be better off without me? I fantasized about renting an apartment in town and moving out. Maybe a little distance would calm things down, help me be more civil with the ones I loved. It wasn't logical. But running has always been my favorite way to address shame. Each time I felt disorder or disunity in the house, I nursed this secret fantasy of escape.

One Sunday afternoon after an outburst with Kennedy in front of Gabe and Pierce (an overreaction that was my fault, not hers), Gabe and I went on a Vespa ride to downtown Leipers Fork. We parked, walked down the street, ducked under an outdoor amphitheater stage, and sat on rocking chairs as rain began pelting the roof. After a few minutes, Gabe said in a near whisper, "Babe, do you realize you're pushing the kids away?" He described how my overreactions felt damaging to the kids and expressed concern that I didn't realize what I was doing.

The truth? I could absolutely see how my mood swings were pushing everyone away, and I felt powerless to stop it. Up to that point, Gabe's pointing out my faults and agreeing with the kids only deepened the wound. It was as if they thought I was the worst, and truth be told, I agreed.

I stared at the stage floor, desperate to explain my actions, but I couldn't. In that amphitheater, when I was at the end of my rope, the Holy Spirit gave me words for the emotions I was feeling: *I am broken. The kind of broken that is beyond repair.* When those words surfaced, I felt as if I was choking. Through tears, I confessed the hardest truth, "I'm afraid I cannot change."

If I've ever seen the mercy of Jesus, it was then. Gabe hugged me, holding me close. He whispered, "We're all broken. You're just more aware of it."

His words hung in the air on that cold, rainy Sunday. I held them as he held me. Rain bounced off the roof above us, a cleansing cadence to my weary and shame-filled heart. Drop by drop, the exhaustion of striving at home began to drain from my body. For the first time in weeks, I let my guard down. I realized then that when the world shut down, I wasn't ready. I had become so accustomed to striving in my work that I simply transferred that muscle memory to home. My family wasn't as forgiving as the workplace, where I could hide stress in a new city as I spoke to new people every single week. At home, my family saw the whole picture—the nonstop pace, the unnecessary burdens, the taking on pressure and putting it on others, the ways I didn't feel permission to stop.

THERE'S A FINE LINE WE CROSS WHERE OUR WORK BECOMES OUR WORTH.

There's a fine line we cross where our work becomes our worth. This is true, whether it's your vocation or the work of being the perfect role model at home. It's so subtle, invisible even, that you rarely see it when it happens. One day you awaken after a decade of sleepless nights, your body so weary you want to quit. You forget why you started in the first place, with no more gas in the tank to keep going. That was me. The adrenaline of obligation became my currency, the way I lived my everyday life.

In the moments after my confession, the words of Jesus broke through: "I won't lay anything *heavy or ill-fitting* on you. Keep company with me and you'll learn to live freely and lightly" (Matthew 11:29–30 MSG, emphasis added).

Somewhere along the way, I had made work a garment that no longer fit. The pace, the platform, the chronic need to push became too much. When it all came to a screeching halt, I created new pressures at home because, evidently, I'm a glutton for pressure. I honestly can't remember a time in my life when I didn't feel some form of pressure, put on by others or by myself. It was my uniform of choice. If I survived the pressure, I felt strong. I was enough. I was worthy of love because I *earned* it.

What a heartbreaking way to live!

My confession, "I am broken," and the grace offered in response, marked the moment everything began to change. For the first time in a long time, I could breathe. I could surrender.

Recognizing the Shame

My confession on that rainy Sunday was a turning point in my spiral of shame, the pattern I'd lived with for decades. In the mornings that followed, I began to read *The Soul of Shame* by Curt Thompson on our front porch, underlining and writing notes on almost every page. I'd never seen myself as a person of shame, but I would soon discover why I was so prone to try to control everything, why I ran and hid when that strategy didn't work, why I shut down in conflict, why I wanted to escape.

The lie of shame whispers, "There is something inherently wrong with you." You're not enough and never will be, so you exhaust yourself trying to prove otherwise. Shame roots in your past and reminds you of all the times your best efforts failed. It taunts in your present to push harder, and still, it threatens you that you'll fall short in the future. Shame leaves you with a sense of being trapped and powerless and having no agency to change. That's not even the worst part. We spend so much time avoiding shame that we often don't recognize it until it's almost too late. That's how it was for me.

How early did I begin my cycle of shame? I don't know exactly.

Curt Thompson helped me understand that we first develop a *sense of shame* in our earliest years. Children come into the world with the primal question, "Who can I trust?" and spend the rest of their lives seeking and finding answers to that question. Our hearts are drawn to acceptance and repelled by rejection. With repeated exposure to rejection, we more permanently encode shame responses. These shame responses are like muscles—the more we use them, the more easily they fire later in life, even when activated by the most minor or unrelated stimuli.[1]

OUR HEARTS ARE DRAWN TO ACCEPTANCE
AND REPELLED BY REJECTION.

As I read Thompson's words, it was as though he were describing my life. I'd been raised to achieve, to succeed. I'd been raised to create a sense of order too. Each time I failed, each time I didn't quite measure up, I was a disappointment to someone. Those many, many disappointments encoded a shame response deep in me. I never realized it before that moment, but if my shame response were an actual muscle, I'd be able to lift my car with it. It's no wonder shame took over as my vocation shifted to the home, as chaos around us set in. I was faced with my family each day, wondering if I was a good enough wife and mother. My shame-response muscle was doing what it was trained to do.

Perhaps you're reading this and wondering, *How do I know if I'm responding in shame? What does a shame response look like?* For decades, I found myself in the middle of conversations where I felt overpowered by shame. My heart would beat rapidly, my breathing would become shallow, and I'd begin to shut down. I didn't have language for it. So I avoided those hard conversations, and in the exceptional moments when I couldn't, I began to avoid the people who brought on those feelings of shame altogether. You can't avoid your family, right? This is why lockdowns exposed fragile marriages and vulnerable relationships with our children. We were forced to face uncomfortable responses we could no longer escape. Why do our bodies feel such a palpable sense of shame? Curt Thompson explains:

> When I experience shame, I find it virtually impossible to turn my attention to something other than what I am feeling. . . . I am not able to think coherently, and my logical processes, which usually help me make good choices, are unavailable to regulate my right brain, from which all of the emotion is pouring.

> Furthermore, my memory is inundated with old, implicit network activity, recollections of other times I have felt this, and I am unable to marshal the necessary memories of strength and confidence I desperately need at the moment. *Shame is overtaking me.* I then begin to construct a narrative that predicts a bleak and pessimistic future. I am unable to tell the whole story, certainly not one in which I am loved by God unconditionally and life, in the end, will be okay. My state of mind is fully disrupted, and transitioning back to one of coherence and peacefulness requires enormous effort. I can only see myself as being intolerable to others, and I sense the impossibility that this feeling will ever end.[2]

You too, Curt? I thought it was just me.

It was the first time I had discovered words for something I couldn't describe. Being seen by a colleague who risked vulnerability made me feel known. Curt was a friend. He had collaborated with me in countless ways, hosting podcasts and retreats on emotional health, but the day I read his words about shame marked a liberation of sorts; a declaration that there must be another way.

When I finally acknowledged the weight of my shame, when I spoke the words, "I am broken," it was more than the acknowledgment of the words. I had a very real physical response that accompanied those words when they came out. Closing throat, shallow breathing, accelerated heart rate. Shame is intrinsic to what we sense emotionally—see, think, and feel. In the confession, the physiological response changed. It was as if I was throwing off a weight. I wanted to live in that weightlessness forever.

I began to pay attention to the patterns of shame my body was revealing. Conversations when others would divert their eyes, or I would divert my own eyes, when questioned or confronted with something uncomfortable. I noticed when I desperately wanted to leave the room, when a disagreement felt too difficult for me to remain. I recognized conflicts that sparked shame, when I believed it was my fault or I couldn't do anything right or maybe everyone would be better off without me. I also perceived times when I wanted to escape, go to my closet, shut the door, sit in the quiet. Sometimes cry, sometimes blame, always alone. Each time I enabled this coping mechanism to calm myself, I reinforced the stronghold of shame. But if I could discern the threat of shame sneaking up on me, I could resist and move forward in renewed strength.

Armed with this new information, I began to respond differently. It's one thing to feel powerless in my shame, quite another to uncover the truth that sets me free. When I sensed shame coming on, I would confront those lies with truth. *You are LOVED. You are SAFE. You don't have to RUN and HIDE.* I began to pause, take deep breaths, and exhale slowly to calm my mind. This helped me stop running from difficult conversations when the tension mounted. The pause allowed time to regroup, ask questions, and seek to understand the intention behind what was said.

When I felt negative emotions recurring in hard conversations with Gabe or the kids, I used an approach recommended by my counselor. I responded by saying, "I don't believe this was your intention, but when you said [this or that], I felt [insert negative emotion]." It validated what was said and how it was received without assuming motives. It kept me from putting them on the defensive simply because they had inadvertently triggered my shame response.

Further, these practices deepened my relationship with Gabe. We banned the words *always* and *never* in statements such as, "This is what you always do," or "You never [such and such]." These loaded words are full of character assassination, and they often come from positions of shame. They assume the worst about the other based on a history of failed attempts to reconcile or on our attempts to shift blame. Removing these phrases from our vocabulary gave us the grace to remember that both of us are good-willed people who fell in love for reasons that still exist.

With these empowering strategies, my window of tolerance increased over the subsequent weeks and months. I learned through practice that the antidote to shame is the willingness to be vulnerable and expose it. Shame's fear of exposure must be turned on its head. It worked for me, it worked for Curt Thompson, and it will work for you as well. Wherever you are in your journey to overcome shame, know that the first step is naming what is broken and then believing you are not condemned. Vulnerability is the kryptonite to shame.

What a liberating way to live!

Resilience Requires Recognizing

Shame keeps us locked in negative spirals. It affects our bodies, robbing us of strength. It also affects our relationships, condemning those who trigger our shame response as the enemy. You've felt this too? Perhaps you're wondering, *Can I truly be resilient if I'm constantly responding in shame?*

For me, my shame response revolved around measuring up, being enough, doing enough. For you, it might be something different. Perhaps you carry the shame of a hidden addiction or secret habit. Maybe you feel the shame of broken relationships. Maybe there's shame from some past trauma in your life, abuse that wasn't your fault.

When you take the time to recognize your shame and find someone you can be vulnerable with—a counselor, pastor, priest, or loved one—you'll find new strength to approach shame physically, emotionally, and psychologically. You are taking the necessary steps toward healing, strength, and resilience.

REFLECTIONS ON RESILIENCE

1. Spend about thirty minutes reflecting on potential areas of shame in your life. It won't be comfortable, but hang in there. Write down those areas of shame.

2. Examine how your body responded as you reflected on those areas of shame. Did your skin get hot? Did you grow short of breath? Did your heart pound or your ears ring? Be specific.

3. Name the person you intend to share this shame with, whether a counselor, loved one, or minister.

INVITE OTHERS IN

CHAPTER FIVE

INVITE OTHERS IN

Be slow to fall into friendship; but when thou art in,
continue firm and constant.

SOCRATES

It's one thing to confess my sin and shame to Gabe and invite him into my deepest places of pain. He's my husband of twenty-five years who knows me better than anyone else, including myself on some days. As I invited him into the raw and fragile places of my life, I found the palpable healing that comes when nothing is hidden. We felt a new level of intimacy—less reacting, more listening and learning. This inspired me to press further. Did I bring a similar level of vulnerability into my friendships? Did my closest friends know my struggles?

After some reflection, I determined to invite others in. I simply made a commitment to be both honest and honoring of others in my response if someone asked. I would no longer look away and choke out the word, "Fine," or worse, "Great!" when I could offer a truer, more vulnerable response. I made it my aim to make eye contact with integrity where the inside matched the outside and to give others the safety to do the same.

The only way I could be this raw and real on the regular was if I'd already done it first before God. The Lord puts all our hardships in perspective with love when we cast our anxieties on him (see 1 Peter 5:7). He tells us to count it *joy* (yes, you heard that right) when trials come because facing trials makes us perfect and complete, lacking nothing (see James 1:2–4). He then begins to comfort us so we can comfort others (see 2 Corinthians 1:4). I decided to put true vulnerability to the test.

Deciding to Get Honest

One Wednesday in late February I gathered with friends to celebrate another birthday. Over winter soup, fresh sourdough bread, kale salad, and Julie's favorite birthday sprinkle cake from Baked on 8th—the birthday girl should always choose the cake—we laughed till our stomachs hurt, something I hadn't done since . . . when? We toasted and celebrated our favorite things about Julie. Then we started sharing life updates.

We'd been apart for months and needed a good bit of catching up, so I asked questions, not sure if I'd be able to keep it together if I had to share. Good friends won't let you stay silent though. They knew me well. Everyone turned my direction, and it was clear they wanted an update. Before I could get a full sentence out, I broke down. When I found my words, I said, "It's been the hardest winter I can remember." As I cried, they surrounded me.

We were in an extended gray winter in Nashville, and I couldn't get out from under the fog of it. Our first snow fell on December 1, and by mid-January, we'd had three major snowfalls that shut down our schools and city for days. It was the damp kind of winter that chills you to the bone, where you can't get warm unless you're in front of a roaring fire. There were glimpses of sunny days, but those passed with what seemed like perpetual waves of cloud-covered cold fronts. As the months wore on, I felt the familiar ghost over my shoulder—seasonal affective disorder.

These friends, who are very good at gently asking all the right questions, wanted details. *What challenges have I been facing? Do I feel shame?* Sure, I felt stalled, apathetic, lost. Yes, small things took all my energy. I worked mostly from home, the house was unruly, and it felt like a success to take my daily walk in the woods or read a brain book—a book that helps me understand what's happening in my own mind. But depressed? Yes. That's exactly how I felt. It took friends holding up a mirror for me to see and speak that truth.

I didn't feel attacked by their questions; I felt guided. Through their kindness, I was able to acknowledge that I was feeling the symptoms of depression. I hadn't struggled with depression since my dad passed away four years earlier and our first move to New York City eight years before that. Since I hadn't said any of this out loud to anyone other than Gabe, I wasn't sure how it would be received. My friends stayed with me. They kept asking and listening, and between bites of birthday sprinkle cake, something surfaced from the deep. I couldn't stop crying, and it wasn't the gentle kind of cry either. It was a guttural grief I couldn't pinpoint until I felt led to the source of my pain. As I verbally processed with my friends, I was able to invite them in.

I began to explain that the slow months and prolonged winter had robbed me of the energy of my vocation, both inside and outside the home. I was no longer the green, fresh writer and speaker I'd once been. I wasn't creating, cooking, or connecting with my family either. I'd given everything to both callings of a working mom, to the point where I was just flat-out exhausted. Each winter, I persevered through the motions but began to feel empty, tempted to hide or retreat. In those slower, dark months when I wasn't traveling or writing as much, I felt discouraged and despairing. I came to realize I was burned-out.

The following week there was another birthday, another group of women. This time, I was going out with longtime friends who had moved to Franklin from New York City. Four of us carpooled downtown, and Vik, who sat next to me in the back seat, asked how I was doing. I briefly shared how this had been a harder winter than the past several years, but this time the news didn't feel so heavy. Because I'd shared my pain the week before, I could better articulate it. It turns out that each woman in the car said she'd had similar struggles that particular winter, and they shared why. Some were new to the city. Others had ongoing sickness. Some missed outdoor exercise. We all acknowledged that some seasons are harder than others for reasons we can't initially explain, but when we share the struggle, we make encouraging connections and feel known.

I kept practicing inviting others in, and in turn they invited me in. A couple weekends later, I met three friends in Colorado for a work trip. We arrived a day early so we could catch up on the past six months. We dove in deep and fast, sharing what God had been doing in our lives. One friend shared ongoing months of sporadic health issues that were crippling her creative writing, without any answers or resolution. Another had ended a long relationship she had fully embraced for almost a year and was trying to process her grief. The third friend was in the middle of a life transition that was changing everything. Even with new ventures on the horizon, she was grieving the end of an era for her entire family. This time, sharing my own struggles was even easier.

Three different encounters with three different communities pulled me out of the deep well of sadness springing from the winter months. It wasn't that any of these connections provided answers or solutions. In fact, it was quite the opposite. All these friends were curious, pressing in with insightful questions, and I did the same for them.

In this Socratic method of asking and listening, conversing, asking again without motive or agenda, we practiced the ministry of empathy and presence. We didn't leave *fixed* after those gatherings; we left with something far greater—the gift of being *with* each other, a *withness* that helped each of us find the courage to keep going.

It has taken me several decades to understand I don't really need answers to every life problem. When life goes sideways, I need to be met with eye contact, curiosity, a listening ear, attentiveness, and withness. I need to be reminded that I'm not crazy and I'm never alone.

The Connection between Empathy and Resilience

Psychological research has shown that both giving and receiving empathy promote psychological health and help us forge connection, reduce stress, and prevent burnout.[1]

For starters, empathy breeds connection. When we put ourselves in someone else's shoes, we're able to hear their story and connect our story with theirs. This shared vulnerability forges connection and offers insights into both our life experience and theirs. By doing this, we learn to regulate our own emotions, thereby improving our response to stress.

Elizabeth Segal, PhD, writes,

> Empathy is about feeling and understanding the experiences of others. It connects you to other people in deep and meaningful ways. While it may be centered on figuring out what is going on for the other person, in that process, you nurture the important human need for connection and attachment. Empathy is the way that we feel understood and reciprocate those feelings. "I hear you" means something important is being exchanged between two people, and that gives us a sense of connection. And being connected to others is good for our well-being.

She continues:

> When we fully engage in empathy, we draw on skills for emotion regulation. In doing so, we are also controlling emotions that can be stressful. Thus, the side benefit from being fully engaged empathically is that we can be exercising good control over our emotions, taking care of our own stress. . . .

> The higher a person's empathy skills, the lower their job burnout. This means that when we build our empathic abilities, we also build our skills at handling difficult work situations, we communicate with others in more effective ways, we understand

others, and we feel better understood. And when we are in that good space at work, we communicate with others in ways that promote collaboration.[2]

Her words about job burnout resonated with me. Perhaps my on-ramp to exhaustion was accelerated by my inability to voice my limits and hear the needs of those around me. Many days, we put our head down and do the work because deadlines demand it. I didn't have the margin to create margin. I didn't pause long enough to take inventory and ask what was right, wrong, confused, and missing, as I wrote about in *Rhythms of Renewal*.[3] Soul care takes continued effort. Life inventory exists for each season because the temptation remains to add "one more thing" when we're optimistic, only to be reminded we're creatures with limits who crave God's presence, the source of soul rest.

How God Models Withness

From the opening pages of Scripture, God shows how he wants to be *with* us. In the Garden of Eden, God walked with Adam and Eve in the cool of the evening. In the exodus, God showed Israel his presence by leading them through the desert as a pillar of fire by night and a pillar of cloud during the day. In the Gospels, Jesus promised his disciples, "Surely I am with you always, to the very end of the age" (Matthew 28:20). In the book of Revelation, John wrote, "God's dwelling place is now among the people, and he will dwell with them. They will be his people, and God himself will be with them and be their God" (Revelation 21:3). See? From the creation story in Eden to the promise of the Holy Spirit dwelling in us when Christ ascended, God has always promised to be fully present with us—in our shame, in our redemption, in our future hope.

It isn't just that God promised to be with us. Through the person of Jesus, he demonstrated his need for others in the midst of his own pain. Missions expert Sonny Guild writes:

> Presence is important. Jesus, on the night he was to face his greatest test, went out to pray. Mark says he was "overwhelmed with sorrow to the point of death" (Mark 14:34). He asked Peter, James, and John to go with him. His one request of them was to stay and keep watch. Their presence was needed by our Lord. I am not sure I understand why. Perhaps this illustrates one of the powerful and meaningful ways we minister to overwhelmed people. To know someone else cares and is there with you is the critical need of the moment.[4]

Even Jesus himself asked for presence in his moment of pain, sorrow, and despair. If Jesus needed that presence, don't we?

Over the course of three encounters with friends who allowed me to share my burden and invited me into theirs, I got the point. God showed me that in our sadness, all of us need someone to be *with* us. It's *with*ness that allows us to unpack our baggage and provides people to help carry the load. Ultimately, this withness enables something springlike to come to the interior of our soul. It thaws the winter of our hearts. It gives us fresh strength and the ability to carry on. It increases our resilience.

We were not made to suffer alone. When we share our pain with friends or family members who commit to walk with us through our darker seasons, a shift happens. We're able to walk another mile, make it another day. Withness allows us to move from surviving to thriving in our everyday lives.

Empathy Creates Resilience

Maybe you've found yourself in a place of deep depression or sadness. Maybe you feel anxious. Maybe you simply feel as if you're at a crossroads and you don't know exactly what to do. Maybe you even have a dream, but you're not sure you can pursue it. If that's you, know this: you are less resilient when you bottle it up.

When we receive empathy, we exercise parts of our brain that make us emotionally healthier, stronger, and better able to withstand the difficulties of life. When we intentionally engage in empathetic exchange, we become more like God, the creator of witness. In these ways, we ultimately become stronger, more equipped to withstand life's storms. In a word, we become more resilient.

Give vulnerability and empathy a chance. Invite others into your struggle and enter their struggles too. In doing so, you'll find that these exchanges lead to healing, which brings greater resilience.

REFLECTIONS ON RESILIENCE

1. Consider those in the Gospels who shared their struggle with Jesus. Write down as many stories as you can. How did Jesus respond? How was their resilience increased in the sharing?

2. Can you think of a time when you struggled with shame, anxiety, depression, or addiction and then shared it with a trusted person? How did you feel after you shared?

3. Can you name some hidden struggle in your life now? Confess it to Jesus and then write the name of a safe person you will share that struggle with.

CHAPTER SIX

THE RHYTHM OF CONFESSION

THE RHYTHM OF CONFESSION

*The desperate need of our time is not for successful
Christians, popular Christians, or winsome Christians; it's
for deep Christians. And the only way to become a deep
Christian is through the inner excavation called confession.*
TYLER STATON

My shame breakthrough taught me how I'd carried so much
adversity for so long, how its weight became unbearable,
and how my body suffered physiologically because of it. That's not
all it taught me. As I recognized pain more readily, I learned to
counter with vulnerability and to invite others in. I found a profound strength in the solidarity of empathy and presence. I began
to learn to offload shame more often. How? By naming the pain
and bringing it to light the *minute* I felt it. Put simply, by practicing
the rhythm of confession.

At first, I had no idea how welcome this confession practice would
be among my family, friends, and community. Would it make

them uncomfortable or cause them to distance themselves? To my surprise and delight, my friends not only welcomed this raw vulnerability with open arms, but they also reciprocated. This rhythm of confession became a rhythm of healing. Each time I would share a hardship and then talk about the rescue of God from my shame, people would respond with their own vulnerability, inviting God to set them free. It turned out that the insecurity I fought so desperately to hide became the freedom I could not keep still about. Isn't that the redemption of God? His strength is made perfect in and through our weakness, because God's power is revealed in our confession (see 2 Corinthians 12:9)!

THIS RHYTHM OF CONFESSION BECAME A RHYTHM OF HEALING.

This practice of confession cultivated a renewed resilience in every way. Gabe noted I became more gracious, patient, and content with my limitations as a wife, mother, and friend. Honesty came more naturally, and a calm ensued. Talking to God became a natural and effortless cadence throughout each day during intentional moments of transition. I felt more myself, more satisfied, more able to navigate the trials of the day with a sense of peace, calm, and reason. The Spirit was on full display in my heart in ways I had not encountered in years, maybe decades. Freedom follows when you have nothing left to hide.

Scripture came alive again too. I read with eyes wide open, and I saw how the rhythm of confession helps us combat shame and how God gave us confession—both to God and each other—for healing to be possible (James 5:16). Sometimes we like to keep our confession between just us and God. I've learned through count-less moments in ministry that the minute someone confesses to another person where a break in relationship exists, chains are broken. Honesty is the best form of connection and healing, both with God and with one another.

Confession Is the Foundation

If you've spent time in the church, you've probably learned that sin separates. It starts by separating us from God. But if we confess our sins and the shame that goes with them, God is faithful and just and will forgive us our sins and cleanse us from all unrighteousness (see 1 John 1:9).

Sin also separates us from one another, as my kids and Gabe can attest. It doesn't just separate us because it causes pain to others; it also separates us because in our shame, we withdraw from others. Loneliness follows that withdrawal. And depression follows loneli-ness. Then we find ourselves sick to the core, just like I was when I fantasized about moving away. Confession is so important because it restores relationship with Christ, the church, and those closest to us.

Finally, sin separates us from ourselves. We lose touch with our pain and deepest longings, and our reactions to them. In the Psalms, we see David examining his heart and, by extension, modeling how we should examine our own hearts. In Psalm 139, he writes, "Search me, God, and know my heart; test me and know my anx-ious thoughts. See if there is any offensive way in me, and lead me in the way everlasting" (vv. 23–24). We need the Holy Spirit to connect our heads back to our hearts so that we might participate in the rhythm of confession.

David had murdered and committed adultery, but the reason he was considered a man after God's own heart was that he withheld nothing from God. He invited God to examine his heart, asking the Holy Spirit to illuminate what David couldn't see. God always reveals the places he wants to heal. Once David confessed, he asked to be led away from sin into an abiding life of fruitful abundance.

GOD ALWAYS REVEALS THE PLACES HE WANTS TO HEAL.

Each Sunday, our family gathers with fellow believers to remember Christ through the Eucharist, or what many of us refer to as Communion. We take the bread and wine, as Jesus did at the Last Supper. We repeat the words he spoke to his disciples, and we eat and drink together, remembering his death, burial, and resurrection. We celebrate and give thanks for the salvation Christ brought on the cross. This is a really big deal.

The apostle Paul understood the weight of the Lord's Supper. In fact, he taught that before we eat the bread and drink the wine, we need to examine our hearts, just as David did, and confess our sins. To the church in Corinth, Paul wrote these words:

> So then, whoever eats the bread or drinks the cup of the Lord in an unworthy manner will be guilty of sinning against the body and blood of the Lord. Everyone ought to examine themselves before they eat of the bread and drink from the cup. For those who eat and drink without discerning the body of Christ eat and drink judgment on themselves. That is why many among you are weak and sick, and a number of you have fallen asleep. (1 Corinthians 11:27–30)

This is why I don't take the Eucharist casually. Each of us is invited into this promise. Confession before Communion creates a pathway for healing.

CONFESSION BEFORE COMMUNION
CREATES A PATHWAY FOR HEALING.

In her autobiography, Mother Teresa wrote, "When I see someone sad, I always think, she is refusing something to Jesus."[1] I think of how often I've withheld my burdens from God—regarding my children or marriage or work. I knew these concerns were weighing me down, but maybe I was afraid to let go. Jesus simply wants to take them off our back—the guilt of sin and the weight of shame—and give us a pure heart. The apostle John promises, "If we confess our sins, he is faithful and just and will forgive us our sins and purify us from all unrighteousness" (1 John 1:9). When we surrender and ask for God's forgiveness, we receive the joy that comes with restored relationship and complete freedom with him!

Tell the Truth

Healed bodies and souls become resilient bodies and souls. If we want to be whole, buffered by true resilience, we begin by telling the truth. Consider Frederick Buechner's take:

> What we hunger for perhaps more than anything else is to be known in our full humanness, and yet that is often just what we also fear more than anything else. It is important to tell at least from time to time the secret of who we truly and fully are—even if we tell it only to ourselves—because otherwise we run

the risk of losing track of who we truly and fully are and little by little come to accept instead the highly edited version which we put forth in hope that the world will find it more acceptable than the real thing.[2]

This resonates with the way I used to view confession. Society has normalized a highly edited version of ourselves. We have feeds that share only the most beautiful or celebratory moments. Because we've been trained by the world to accept an edited version of who we are—one that appears stronger, more together, even holier—confession has been seen as a sign of weakness. This avoidance of confession holds us captive to shame, which makes us *actually* weak. Jesus modeled the opposite. He did anything but edit the most vulnerable moments of his life, as the author of Hebrews makes clear:

> During the days of Jesus' life on earth, he offered up prayers and petitions with fervent cries and tears to the one who could save him from death, and he was heard because of his reverent submission. Son though he was, he learned obedience from what he suffered and, once made perfect, he became the source of eternal salvation for all who obey him. (Hebrews 5:7–9)

Jesus is able to empathize with our weakness because he was weak. He was tempted in every way, just as we are, yet he didn't sin. Therefore we can cry out and confess with confidence, resting in the assurance that we will receive God's abundant mercy and grace in our time of need (see Hebrews 4:15–16). Tyler Staton, pastor of Bridgetown Church in Portland, Oregon, writes:

> One of the biggest mistakes we've made in the modern church

is to reimagine spiritual maturity as the need to confess less. . . . True spiritual maturity, though, is the opposite. It's not an ascension; it's an archaeological dig as we discover layer after layer of what was in us all along. Spiritual maturity means more confession, not less. . . . A maturing community is a confessing community—not a church without sin, but a church without secrets.[3]

Here's the thing I don't want you to miss: the enemy dwells in the secret. Our secrets make us hide, and we stay hidden because of shame. Our hiding then breaks relationship both with God and with one another. So the cycle continues. The enemy accuses and gets us to agree.

THE ENEMY DWELLS IN THE SECRET.

What would it look like to be a church without secrets? I cannot fathom it, but I do dream of it, because I know that God's grace is more powerful than our sin. Attaining the peace and power that come through confession begins with you and with me. It begins by asking the Holy Spirit to illuminate whatever is lurking in the dark, with the help of these questions:

What am I withholding from God?

Are there any hidden motives and insecurities?

Am I grieving something I'm not over yet?

Who do I need to talk to about this?

Building resilience begins with confession, first to God and then to one another. We don't hide anything, don't shade the facts, don't make excuses. We confess our brokenness to God and one another *so that* we may be healed. And as we do, as we're healed, we find freedom.

A Word on Forgiveness

I'm thankful we serve a God who welcomes our confession, who promises to forgive us. This promise to forgive demonstrates God's unconditional love—a love that wants us to be set free from the shame and pain of our sin. In many ways, confession and repentance come first because God is ready and willing to restore our broken relationship with him. Unfortunately, it's not always that way with people.

Some of us are so badly wounded we simply feel unable to forgive. If we've engaged in a pattern of harm against another, resentment and bitterness may have set in. Even if we're ready to make it right, that doesn't mean they are ready to forgive.

I have my own history of sinning against others. There were times I repented to God, was forgiven by God, and then was led to confess the harm I did to someone else. Sometimes the walls of bitterness were so high that the relationship still suffered. I've also been the one hurt, unable to extend forgiveness even though I've been forgiven so often by God.

Here's what I've discovered: to restore relationships with others, we need to be willing to confess *and* forgive, just as God in Christ forgave us. Scripture says God will forgive us in the same way we forgive others (see Matthew 6:14). This is convicting! So if I don't forgive others when they confess to me, how will God respond to my confession?

Further, I need to forgive those who never confess or even ask for forgiveness. This is how I keep a clean heart before God, free of bitterness where the enemy can get a foothold to make further advances (see Ephesians 4:27). I'm not responsible for another's confession, but I *am* responsible for a tender heart of forgiveness. My freedom from the enemy's future schemes depends on it.

In the end, all of our pain results from broken relationships with Christ and others. When we're honest about this from the start, we begin to see that the pathway to healing, freedom, and resilient community is found in confession and forgiveness. We begin to rebuild the pathways of connection and intimacy with people, freed from brokenness and shame. In the next chapter, we'll see how this kind of freedom is paramount to living in a resilient community.

REFLECTIONS ON RESILIENCE

1. Spend some time opening yourself up to God. Ask him to examine your heart and show you any areas of sin or shame that need to be confessed. Write down those areas in a journal.

2. Commit to the work of confessing sin to God and to those you've hurt. Write down a plan for confessing, including a time and place for confession and what you will say.

3. Is there anyone you need to forgive? Write their names on a piece of paper, along with why you feel hurt by them; then ask God to give you the same forgiveness for them he has given you. If you feel led, go to them. Clear the air. Bless them.

RULE TWO

SHIFT THE NARRATIVE

RENEW YOUR MIND

Narratives help us make sense of the stories we tell ourselves. They collect and organize myriad events, experiences, and encounters into a single story. This story then shapes our understanding of who we are, where we've been, and where we are going. Our narrative becomes a powerful influence on the way our mind perceives each moment and informs the way we respond.

We live in a world of many competing narratives. There are competing political narratives, with each side turning the other into a villain. There are competing narratives in the arena of health—do we pursue holistic or conventional medicine? Even in the church, some pursue a progressive vision of Christianity while others hold to the conservative teachings of the past.

These narratives impact our daily lives, but they don't affect us nearly as much as the narratives we tell ourselves about our own lives. If we're going to be people of resilience, we'll need to know how to preach to ourselves, retrain our brains, and know the truth. When we do these things, we strengthen our minds and our spirits. We become people who recognize truth and live into it, thereby making us more resilient.

PREACH
TO YOURSELF

PREACH TO YOURSELF

You get to decide what you say to yourself.

SADIE ROBERTSON

As spring unfolded and the deep ache of sadness lifted, Gabe and I prepped for our spring retreat. We began hosting these retreats in the fall of 2020 when people were gathering in smaller numbers, and this time, we were eager to share our favorite Colorado destination—Lost Valley Ranch—with a great group of people.

If you've read *Rhythms of Renewal*, you may recall how I overcame my fear of horses at Lost Valley. After I defeated that fear, my confidence in horseback riding grew to the point where I came to love horses more than just about any other animal. They're powerful, but once I learned to trust and work with them, I felt a sense of connection with the horse, a freedom. I looked forward to sharing that freedom with others.

On the two-hour commute from the Denver airport, my anticipation grew, and it was almost unbearable as we turned onto the dusty cliff-hanger road that wound around the side of a mountain—equal parts terrifying and exhilarating. A few miles later, we crossed into the valley and drove over the cattle guard into the entrance of the ranch. It's hard to describe the feeling that came over me, but if pressed, I'd have to say it was a sense of coming home.

For years, our friends Tony and Brooke gave us the same instructions before we came to the ranch: leave behind whatever is plaguing you and receive this space as a sanctuary for refreshment, restoration, and rest. Lost Valley is a nostalgic reminder of the way life used to be—wild and untamed in the vast setting of the majestic mountains—before the lure of technology convinced us that life was something to be observed rather than experienced. It's one of the only places where I nap most afternoons, a thing I didn't know I was capable of until the first time I visited. It's also one of the rare places without roaming Wi-Fi or television screens. Once you've checked off horseback riding, trail hiking, or an hour or two of fly-fishing, there's nothing more relaxing than retreating to your cabin, settling down with a good book, and drifting off to sleep. That's why we were excited to host new friends for several days of retreat.

We stepped out of our rental car onto a dirt driveway and were greeted by the staff. They'd become our friends over the years, so we exchanged hugs and caught up on life while we worked together to fill gift baskets for each guest. After the baskets were delivered to the rooms, I walked to the corral, greeted the wranglers for the weekend, said hello to my favorite horses—Amigo,

Newcastle, and Shorty—and then retired to our cabin to get ready for opening night.

We gathered that evening, women in our dresses and braids, men in their Wranglers, all of us in boots and hats. After drinks and a little conversation, we went around the room, making space for introductions, and each of us shared a "Hard and Hopeful"—what was hard in the past twelve months and what we hoped to experience during the next three days.

When you open spaces of vulnerability, it's amazing what can happen in an hour. Seventy-five people—seventy-five "Hard and Hopefuls." The couples shared honestly, though they didn't know each other. Some shared feelings of exhaustion, burnout, defeat. Others shared tales of marital struggles. All were hopeful for restoration, healing, rest. This practice of vulnerability shifted beyond connections with each other to connections all around the room.

With transparency, there's no limit to what God can do. God doesn't deny a heart that's expectant. This group embodied that kind of heart. Each person in that room traveled across the country and sacrificed time and resources because they needed to see God do a work and believed he would honor his promise to reward those who diligently seek him: "And without faith it is impossible to please God, because anyone who comes to him must believe that he exists and that he rewards those who earnestly seek him" (Hebrews 11:6).

GOD DOESN'T DENY A HEART THAT'S EXPECTANT.

It wasn't just the attendees who arrived with this perspective. Gabe and I were just as eager for the move of God in our marriage and family. We want to endure with what pastor Eugene Peterson called a "long obedience in the same direction," and we know this kind of long obedience—which is nothing short of true resilience—doesn't just happen.[1] It must be cultivated and nurtured in dedicated space. We brought our "Hard and Hopefuls" too.

Following dinner, dancing under the stars, and a few pockets of conversation that went deep into the night, we slept hard. Once we awakened the following morning, we didn't waste any time. We gathered to kick off our opening session with our marriage therapists, Bill and Laurie Lokey. Laurie has been my counselor since 2015, just a year into my time in Nashville. She's had extensive training in trauma recovery and created an individual intensive therapy model for those dealing with trauma called "trauma stage processing." Bill became Gabe's therapist a few years later, and together they've led us into new levels of healing as we celebrate twenty-five years of marriage.

We were excited for them to share their wisdom with our new guests at the retreat, but as Bill began speaking, he revealed an insight none of us saw coming. He had been diagnosed with metastatic bone cancer four years earlier, which he has fought valiantly through exploratory treatments at MD Anderson with a grateful smile and inspiring faith. Bill and Laurie never wavered in their trust in God, and he shared how they honored their feelings surrounding each setback through these recent years tethered to family and community. They kept their counseling practice going and tried to live every moment they had to the full.

Last fall, the narrative shifted. The doctors told Bill he only had one more Christmas, and so he needed to prepare for a decline until his last days. While he knew the end was inevitable, this news provoked a languishing in his spirit, a sadness that overcame him. It took him a few days to identify the source, and then he had an epiphany.

I need to shift the narrative.

While the doctor's prognosis that fall was meant to help them prepare to end well, it also shifted the way Bill saw his cancer. "I realized I went from fighting to live to preparing to die," he said. "And God can't transform a dead sacrifice. He asks us to present our bodies as a living sacrifice." Bill decided that while he had no idea when his last day on earth would come, he would continue to be a living sacrifice for God and would take and use each moment in whatever way God saw fit. He would wake up every morning prepared to live, with breath in his lungs. In a moment when no one else's words could bring clarity, he began to preach to himself.

His family came on board with the new narrative and decided they wouldn't waste a moment; they would take every opportunity to encourage Bill to live. They planned and then gathered within a few weeks to create a "celebration of life" moment that Bill could enjoy—hearing from his kindred friends and family members about the amazing contributions he had made to each of them. He was reminded that until his last breath, he has even more to give. Bill's mind was being renewed as he encountered the truth and mustered up the courage to embrace life every single day.

The power of Bill preaching to himself was transformative to my understanding of what a life lived well looks like, no matter the circumstance. As I write these words, Bill is still preaching to himself. He's actively counseling with Laurie as he continues to fill his days with meaningful work. In fact, a few months after our retreat, Bill created a new course titled "Resilient Love," which sold out immediately and had a waiting list. Toward the end of the program, Bill contracted COVID pneumonia and was hospitalized, and yet he continued to write and tweet the program. Even as Bill was recovering in the hospital, the course attendees were able to follow along. Through Bill's weakness, God's perfect strength provided incredible healing for everyone. What a testimony!

Bill continues on pain medication, and we surround him in prayer for new treatments that might prolong his life. Scripture tells us our days are numbered and none of us know when we will take our last breath (see Job 14:5; Psalms 90:10–12; 139:16; James 4:14). No matter the outcome, Bill has come to embody a truth: God can *always* revive an available heart.

Offer Your Bodies

The experience with Bill Lokey that day captured exactly why we love to host retreats. It forces us to enter new spaces, be present and embodied, be physically active, and engage with others we never would have met had we stayed comfortably at home. We use the time to work through exercises that ask everyone to stop, reflect, and take action—whether through our "Take Inventory"[2] tool or through noting the gray areas in a marriage relationship that need to be addressed with intentional conversation. It's normal to fall into mental routines that begin to stick. We start to believe things can never change, but those are the moments when we need to be reawakened to the truth and jolted to our senses.

Romans 12:1–2 inspires me to be resilient, just like Bill Lokey, all the way to the end:

> Therefore, I urge you, brothers and sisters, in view of God's mercy, to offer your bodies as a living sacrifice, holy and pleasing to God—this is your true and proper worship. Do not conform to the pattern of this world, but be transformed by the renewing of your mind. Then you will be able to test and approve what God's will is—his good, pleasing and perfect will.

For years, I read this challenge to offer our *bodies* as a living sacrifice and never fully grasped it meant our *actual* bodies—our flesh-and-blood, moving, breathing, pulse-pumping bodies. When Scripture is read as metaphor, sometimes we miss what is blatantly obvious—for example, Jesus' command to his disciples to follow him didn't mean, "Jot this down in your journal and ponder what it means to follow"; it meant, "Get up and use your actual legs and come with me to where I am going." Scholars believed he walked more than three thousand miles from town to town in his three years of ministry, and the whole time, he invited his followers to sacrifice their bodies to follow him.[3]

Likewise, getting up, showing up, and presenting our bodies in any type of gathering requires sacrifice—childcare, savings, planning, preparing. Yet this kind of sacrifice runs counter to a digital era. Culture suggests that intimacy is just as possible through a screen; in reality, when we arrive in person, we are practicing a new level of intimacy and vulnerability. This is why the church is urged in Scripture to never forsake meeting together (see Hebrews 10:25).

Paul writes, "Do not conform to the pattern of this world." His assumption is that the natural forces of life will steer our bodies away from sacrifice toward a path that doesn't lead to our flourishing but perhaps instead to our demise. The only way to fight this trajectory is to be transformed. We do this through the renewing of our minds.

Renew Your Minds

Renewing our minds may sound like a foggy idea, so let's get very practical about how we apply this in modern times. The word *mindful*, which means "attentive," has become more in vogue in recent years, and yet mindfulness is consistently modeled in Scripture. The book of Psalms is filled with poetry by writers who were attentive to their longings and emotions. Jesus modeled attentiveness to everyone he encountered, with words of encouragement, food for nourishment, even physical healing. The art of paying attention is a good first step, especially for the Christian who desires to renew their mind. Once we observe our current thoughts and begin to identify and name them, the Bible says we *renew* our minds when we do more than just passively observe our thoughts; to renew our minds is to actively trade our limited thinking for God's perfect and comprehensive thinking.

Psalm 1:1–3 reads, "Blessed is the one . . . whose delight is in the law of the LORD, and who meditates on his law day and night. That person is like a tree planted by streams of water, which yields its fruit in season and whose leaf does not wither." Furthermore, in Jeremiah 17:8, this tree is described as resilient: "They will be like a tree planted by the water that sends out its roots by the stream. It does not fear when heat comes; its leaves are always green. It has no worries in a year of drought and never fails to bear fruit."

We have the potential to fill our minds with truth day and night. When we renew our minds, we become resilient, like a tree planted by water that continues to produce fruit, no matter what storms come its way. I can't help but think of Bill Lokey as I read this powerful truth.

Renewing our minds requires taking account of the thoughts we have, the books we read, the content we let in, and the ideas we've come to trust. We get to decide what we think, how we think, and which inputs we allow in or throw out. In our home, Gabe and I audited the shows we watch, the news sources we trust, and the amount of time spent on both. This audit resulted in the cancellation of several streaming services that offered up nonsense or tempted us toward mindlessness. We gained time back into our day, and our perspectives and attitudes became more positive. Taking such an inventory is a great way to assess how your mind is being shaped.

I've had to evaluate how often I approach my days by leading with the negative: *What can I change?* When I start my day speaking fatigue and exhaustion over myself, I miss the chance to receive God's mercies that are new every morning. When I begin with a grateful heart, I gain the resilience that offers strength. I've had to preach to myself, *Rebekah, let's walk out the door and treat the day as if it's already redeemed. Reject any temptation to despair and choose to trust and live fully.*

This can be easier said than done. Preaching to ourselves requires a knowledge of what is true, a security that our identity comes from Christ, and the wisdom to discern when toxic thinking is invading our mental space. We build a resilient life by taking account of toxic thoughts and retraining our brains to think differently.

WE BUILD A RESILIENT LIFE BY TAKING ACCOUNT
OF TOXIC THOUGHTS AND RETRAINING
OUR BRAINS TO THINK DIFFERENTLY.

What Truth Do You Need to Preach to Yourself?

Do you struggle with negative thoughts? Are you tempted to focus on your brokenness, failure, and weakness? Do you dwell on your anxieties? To find resilience, you begin by shifting the narrative. Dr. Daniel Amen urges us to wake up each morning and say out loud, "Today is going to be a great day!"[4] Though this may sound like a stretch, try to say it out loud anyway. If you repeat it enough, you'll begin to laugh at yourself. Once you laugh out loud, you'll begin to believe it.

Remember that God has made you for a specific time and has given you a purpose. Remember your purpose, and design your day around it. Press into the ongoing invitation to believe that God is faithful to complete what he begins. Preach this truth to yourself daily. When you do, you'll move with strength, courage, and confidence. You'll be unwavering in the storms of life.

REFLECTIONS ON RESILIENCE

1. What narrative have you believed about your life? What needs to shift in order for the way you see your future to be transformed?

2. How has your life inadvertently been conformed to the ways of this world?

3. In what practical ways can you renew your mind?

RETRAIN
YOUR BRAIN

RETRAIN YOUR BRAIN

The idea that the brain can change its own structure and function through thought and activity is, I believe, the most important alteration in our view of the brain since we first sketched out its basic anatomy and the workings of its basic component, the neuron.

DR. NORMAN DOIDGE

Gabe and I were sound asleep when our sixteen-year-old daughter, Kennedy, burst into our room at one thirty in the morning. Gasping for air and desperate, she cried out, "I need help! I can't get a breath."

I sat up, pulled her close, and calmly but firmly said, "You're okay, Kennedy. This is a panic attack. Your body feels crazy, but you know what to do. We're going to breathe through it. Ready, let's take four slow, deep breaths. In your nose and out of your mouth." I counted out slowly: "1–2–3–4, okay, hold for two counts, then slowly exhale four more counts." We repeated this process a few more times, and with each slow and steady inhale and exhale, her heart rate began to regulate. In just three minutes, her brain began to calm down, and twenty minutes later, we prayed together and sent her back to her room. Crisis averted.

This wasn't Kennedy's first time walking through extreme feelings of anxiety. At just twelve years old, she experienced a racing heart and shortness of breath while away at camp. A new environment triggered her. When the quiet set in and she was left alone with her thoughts, her thinking turned fearful and her body responded. That was the first time we talked about the way panic can set in, the way it can attack your body. We've been having those conversations ever since.

It should come as no surprise that my daughter has been privy to the mental health conversation longer than most children, since I write and speak about my own struggles with anxiety. Whether my challenges have prompted her awareness of these feelings or given her the moxie to walk through them, we'll never know. With more than one in three high school students—her peer group—reporting feelings of depression or anxiety, I wish the younger generation could be empowered with the tools to respond to their mental health challenges just as Kennedy is.[1]

Over the years, Kennedy and I have had ample opportunities to talk through the science of panic. She knows it's her body's natural fear response to a racing heart, a response that sets off a danger alarm in the brain. The amygdala—the fight-or-flight processor—tells her hypothalamus that something is wrong, which notifies the adrenal glands to flood her bloodstream with adrenaline and the stress hormone called cortisol. The adrenaline and cortisol kick the body into survival mode. Her pupils dilate. Her blood sugar spikes. Her mind becomes laser focused on the problem at hand. Her breathing accelerates. Most of the blood drains from her fingers and toes and rushes to her arms and legs, readying them for battle. Kennedy's panic response—a natural response—is just like yours and mine because, just like us, she's only human.

By helping Kennedy understand the science of panic, I've seen her confidence grow in how she responds when the attacks come. No longer afraid she's about to die, she is equipped to work through her response in a different way. Understanding the science is one thing; knowing how to rewire our brains to fend off the trauma is a practice that takes a strategy.

Becoming What You Think

The brain is an amazing organ. Weighing only three pounds, it is the control center for our entire body, containing 100 billion neurons with 100 trillion connections.[2] Information passes between neurons at the speed of 250 miles per hour. Our brains allow us to feel, taste, see, smell, hear, and think, and all that processing power requires approximately 20 percent of the blood and oxygen in our bodies.[3] The more science discovers about the brain, the more we're blown away by the majesty of God's unique design. Though the brain is fully formed by the age of eighteen, changing the way it performs is still possible. If we're going to become resilient people, we can discover and implement ways to change our thinking.

We don't become what we dream; we become what we think. Great thinkers have always known this to be true. René Descartes, the seventeenth-century French philosopher, said, "I think, therefore I am."[4] Ralph Waldo Emerson, the nineteenth-century American essayist and philosopher, is reported to have said, "You become what you think about all day long." Modern books about thinking, such as Napoleon Hill's *Think and Grow Rich* and more recent books such as *Think Again* by Adam Grant, have become bestsellers for a reason.[5] The philosophers and writers understand this truth of human psychology. Our thoughts shape our perspective, our perspective shapes our attitude, and our attitude determines our outcomes.

OUR THOUGHTS SHAPE OUR PERSPECTIVE, OUR PERSPECTIVE SHAPES OUR ATTITUDE, AND OUR ATTITUDE DETERMINES OUR OUTCOMES.

My brain runs my show. Your brain runs your show. If we want to change our lives by developing resilience in the realm of our mental health, it will take a commitment to retraining our brains. The key to overcoming anxiety, depression, and panic begins when we *recognize* how our thoughts drive our physiological response. Scripture is replete with wisdom on the power of the mind to shape our perspective.

> I *meditate on your precepts*
> and consider your ways.
> (Psalm 119:15, emphasis added)

> You will keep in perfect peace
> those *whose minds are steadfast*,
> because they trust in you.
> (Isaiah 26:3, emphasis added)

Finally, brothers and sisters, whatever is true, whatever is noble, whatever is right, whatever is pure, whatever is lovely, whatever is admirable—if anything is excellent or praiseworthy—*think about such things.* (Philippians 4:8, emphasis added)

Therefore, with minds that are *alert and fully sober, set your hope* on the grace to be brought to you when Jesus Christ is revealed at his coming. (1 Peter 1:13, emphasis added)

Be alert and of sober mind. Your enemy the devil prowls around like a roaring lion looking for someone to devour. (1 Peter 5:8, emphasis added)

Scripture illuminates how we think about our circumstances, and where we choose to place our focus will directly impact how we experience life. To develop a resilient mind, we first must take our thoughts captive: "We take captive every thought to make it obedient to Christ" (2 Corinthians 10:5).

How Others Train Our Brains

Unfortunately, trauma negatively impacts our brains and can come from multiple directions. We're impacted not only by childhood experiences, but even world events outside of our control can deteriorate our resilience. History is awash with cautionary tales of authoritarian governments, marketers, and corporations using propaganda to manipulate the masses and shift their thinking. At first blush, it seems impossible to believe that entities with no personal influence in our lives can shape our minds and behavior. But the brain is trainable. It responds to stimuli in predictable ways.

The powers that be know this and take advantage of it. They've learned their tactics from science.

The science of brain training was popularized with the discovery of Pavlovian theory in the 1950s, which proved that the brain is manipulable when subject to fear and scarcity. In 1953, Ivan Pavlov famously trained a dog to respond to the ringing of a dinner bell. After ringing a bell for a prolonged period of time whenever he fed a dog, he discovered that the dog salivated each time the bell rang, even with no food present, demonstrating the brain-to-biology reaction.

Pavlov's work continued on in the field of physiology, where later studies showed that humans are just as trainable as dogs. When the human mind is thrust into fearful circumstances—whether a threatening famine, pending global crisis, or wartime scenario—it becomes susceptible to mass manipulation. Critical-thinking features shut down in an emotionally exhausted state and thus the brain becomes easy to manipulate.

Documentaries such as *The Social Dilemma* have helped expose the way our brains are being manipulated.[6] Whether through the stimuli of a "like" on Instagram that provides a dopamine hit or the exploding confetti vibrations on your watch when you reach ten thousand steps in a day, technology developers have tapped into the power of stimulating our brains to shape behavior in both positive and negative ways.

I wish it weren't the case. When government leaders, social media companies, news outlets, and corporations prey on our mental vulnerabilities as a means of gaining profit or power, they reveal motivations for control. They persuade by using fear, anxiety, and scarcity. No wonder we so often feel at a loss. Here's the good news: We don't have to be manipulated by schemes of the evil one. We can determine how we will perceive and respond to our circumstances. We can recover agency by training our brains.

How to Get Rewired

Left to itself, the brain responds and reacts. Especially when we're young, before our frontal lobes fully develop in our mid-twenties, we are susceptible to irrational thinking and mental confusion. But new developments in neuroscience show we can change the way we think as we age.

In recent decades, scientists, chemists, biologists, and psychologists have discovered that our brains are more malleable in adulthood than previously believed. We're not stuck with the brain behaviors we developed in adolescence. We can *do* something about it. If we don't like the way we think, perceive, or feel, we can change the way our brains process information. We can retrain our brains!

Healing the traumatized, anxious, or panicked brain doesn't have to be complicated. You can take practical steps to retrain your brain. Begin by asking why you are processing information in certain ways and then determine to respond differently. Once you discover your triggers, you can reject the thoughts and feelings that prompt your mind to hijack your body. Then go on to form a plan. A simple set of strategies can help you overcome those thoughts when they return.

For instance, I have a deep and irrational fear of elevators. Because of this, I gear myself up for elevator rides when taking the stairs isn't an option (and sometimes when it is!). I'll take a few seconds to gather my thoughts before I push the button to go up or down. I remind myself, *Rebekah, this elevator has carried hundreds of people up and down all day. You're going to be fine.* Then when I enter the elevator, I stand near the door and avoid the corners where my claustrophobic feelings might rise. As the doors close, I place my thoughts on an entirely different subject—something on my to-do list or an upcoming social occasion I'm anticipating. My most effective thought pattern is to remember *why* I'm in the elevator. When I remind myself of the important objective that this technological tool—an elevator—makes possible, the focus goes off myself and onto the mission. I take a deep breath and anticipate the ding of the opening door.

Consider the routine of my friend Jim Cress. As a marriage counselor and psychologist who understood and even treated clients dealing with their own mental wellness traumas, he found himself experiencing panic attacks on airplanes.

I could relate.

Instead of never flying again—which would hinder his ability to fulfill his life's work—Jim determined to train his brain to think and feel differently when he boards a plane. In his preboarding prayer of surrender, he hands over control and asks Jesus to be with him. The prayer comforts his heart before he steps onto the airplane. Once in his seat, he inserts his earbuds and listens to mindful meditations and worship music to calm his brain. He has also created his own acrostic of the word *EXIT*, so when he sees those letters everywhere, they mean something different for him. The E is for Embracing, the X for Christ, the I for I, and the T for Trust (Embracing Christ I Trust). These routines for resilience provide a way to focus his brain, and now he has mastered the retraining of his brain.

Anxiety or depression may not be your struggle. Are there other addictions you can't seem to overcome? Our friend Seth struggled with alcohol addiction in the years following a personal trauma. When he finally came clean, he entered therapy. His therapist—someone who understood the power of retraining the brain—asked him to explore his emotions through journaling. If Seth were to feel a desire to drink, the therapist suggested that he recite a meaningful prayer until the feeling passed. Seth did just that. His chosen liturgy was an ancient Orthodox prayer: "Lord Jesus Christ, Son of the living God, have mercy on me, a sinner."

Seth made this prayer his anchor when he felt the compulsion for alcohol, and as he repeated it over the course of weeks and months, he found that his ability to resist the temptation increased. He had retrained his brain to replace the desire for alcohol with a desire to connect with God.

A Generation Responding

Our middle-of-the-night episode with Kennedy marked the beginning of her healing journey. Over the past two years, she has developed a resilient response to keep her heart and mind in a healthy place.

For starters, she set out to read Scripture and to journal most days, even when things *weren't* scary. It helped her faith grow *before* she needed it. It's easy to cry out to God in the depths of despair, but Kennedy learned to spend time in his Word simply because she loves him. When she believes and receives the promises of God through worship, her faith grows. She develops a resilience for future moments of adversity.

Second, Kennedy took seriously her responsibility to retrain her brain and build routines for resilience. As her faith grew, she wanted to memorize specific Scriptures to remind her of what's true. With a Bible nearby, when anxiety begins to present itself, she knows exactly what to do. She reminds herself she's been through this before and is going to be okay. Then she begins to pray and recite her favorite verses, such as "Peace I leave with you" and "Do not let your hearts be troubled and do not be afraid" (John 14:27, 28). Psalm 23:4 comforts her: "Even though I walk through the darkest valley, I will fear no evil." And the imagery of God leading her "beside quiet waters" reminds her that God is near (v. 2).

Instead of coming to our room, she makes every effort to stay put in her bed. She's decided that relying on Mom and Dad isn't the best strategy for the future if she's going to have the resilience necessary to fend off the emotions. She turns her attention to praying for others, training her mind to think about someone else. Kennedy has learned that her anxiety increases when she focuses on herself, so she puts the attention on someone else and lets the anxiety or panic roll through.

Like Kennedy, Jim, Seth, or me, you can retrain your brain. You can teach your kids to do this too. How do you start? By recognizing the moments of anxiety, depression, panic, or addiction when they come. Remember what triggers the emotions or behaviors, then determine a plan of attack when those negative emotions and behaviors return.

Part of your plan may include contacting a therapist to help you navigate through a season of acute instability. Create a training plan and stick to it. When you look back, you'll find that your ability to trade negative thinking for mental resilience is a matter of brain training. The payoff will show up when you need it most—even in your darkest hour.

REFLECTIONS ON RESILIENCE

1. Which of your negative thought patterns or reactions to circumstances are most obvious to you?

2. What is a new routine—a simple strategy—you can set in place to retrain your brain's response to being confronted with a negative situation?

3. Which Bible verse or prayer can you memorize to reset your mind during the next moment you experience stress or anxiety?

THE TRUTH THAT SETS FREE

THE TRUTH THAT SETS FREE

I open a Bible, and His plans, startling, lie there barefaced.
It's hard to believe it, when I read it, and I have to come
back to it many times, feel long across those words, make
sure they are real. His love letter forever silences any doubts.
ANN VOSKAMP

Twenty-two has always been Gabe's favorite number. He wore
it on his jersey in his high school football and basketball days,
just like his older brother had. At college, he lived in dorm 22
all four years. You can imagine it was quite a moment when he
flipped through a photo album in his adult years and discovered
that when he was born, his mom occupied room 122 at Virginia
Baptist Hospital. There are a dozen other stories of the number 22
showing up in Gabe's life, and while we don't believe in numerol-
ogy, whenever the number shows up from time to time, it gives us
a little wink.

In the winter of 2022, the number took a deeply negative

connotation. In the same hospital where Gabe's life came into existence, his mother breathed her last breath. The time—2:22 p.m. on January 22, 2022.

Darlene Lyons fought ovarian cancer for more than four years. I'll never forget when Gabe got the initial phone call during a fall break visit with my family in Orlando in October 2017. Darlene and Melvin (Gabe's father) texted both Gabe and me to ask if we could schedule a call that day. It was an odd request, one that made us nervous, so we called them back right away. Within seconds of saying hello, both of them were in tears. She had fought stomach discomfort for months, and her doctor ordered blood tests. This led to further testing, which ultimately revealed that stage 3 ovarian cancer had spread throughout her abdomen. My head began to spin with questions as she continued filling us in on the details.

Risks? Return rate? Oncologist? Surgery? Type of treatment? Side effects? Timeline?

The next few days were a crash course in Darlene's cancer prognosis and treatment. As the mornings and nights blurred together, Gabe did what he does best—research. He went down the rabbit hole of statistics, remission rates, potential outcomes. He spoke with everyone he knew who had any level of experience in the cancer community, both those who made it through the disease and their loved ones who cared for them. I'd never seen him so worried or so committed to finding a solution.

Within days of the diagnosis, surgery with a highly respected doctor was scheduled at the Johns Hopkins Hospital in Baltimore—within driving distance of their hometown. I flew up to see her a day later.

Darlene greeted me with a wave, a weathered smile, and grateful eyes. Before I left, I visited the hospital chapel with Darlene in her wheelchair. She commented to me how beautiful it was. She left the hospital resolved to fight.

And fight she did.

During round one of chemo, she rallied for months. Her CA-125 numbers—the measurement used to determine how active ovarian cancer is in the body—dropped dramatically by spring. Darlene came to visit us on Mother's Day, with a fancy new wig under a pretty pink hat. We attended church where we enjoyed a full slate of festivities for moms, celebrated over lunch, and sat on our front porch talking all afternoon.

Darlene was a wonderful listener and an even better teacher. She shared tender insights on how cancer was coaching her on the meaning of life and on what mattered most, and she pointed to the new ways she was resolving to live. I shared with her how my passion for work had faded after our decision three months earlier to adopt a girl from China—our Joy. I was also reeling from the unexpected passing of my dad a month earlier, and I was caught in an eddy of grief. She said something remarkable that sunny afternoon, something I've quoted countless times ever since: "Rebekah, nothing you are experiencing hasn't been sifted through God's hand."

I stared across the fields from our front porch, a knot forming in my stomach as I processed her words. She was right. I had been hiding from God in my grief, demanding justice for the inner ache. I longed to lean into him the same way I saw her model her trust in God in her pain.

She continued, "I thank God every day for this season because I've never felt closer to him. Each day, I trust him with every test, scan, and treatment, and I'm experiencing his comfort and love in ways I never would have imagined."

I sat there stunned at her peaceful presence while fighting cancer, convicted yet inspired. I'd experienced utter dependence when Cade was born, when God was merciful in the way he drew and held me close. Yet sometimes we know the truth, but we *forget* the goodness of God in the middle of great loss. I needed this reminder from Darlene to trust God again.

Darlene kept her commitment to this level of intimacy with her heavenly Father over the course of the next three years, as she continued to fight round after round with chemo. With each visit, she felt a little weaker and moved a little slower, but we always beheld her brave and joyful face.

Even as the cancer ravaged her body, Darlene continued to spend countless hours making fancy, homemade birthday cards containing handwritten Scriptures and encouragement for every extended family member. She kept filling creative and beautiful photo albums for each grandchild, with her beautiful penmanship journaling each detail. She led Bible studies with women in her church and even took seminary classes in her final two years of life because she wanted to learn everything she could about the Bible. We all watched her live out Psalm 16:8 in real time: "I keep my eyes always on the LORD. With him at my right hand, I will not be shaken."

In November 2021, she and Melvin contracted COVID-19. Melvin recovered; Darlene did not. So four weeks later, the day after Christmas, she was admitted to the hospital. She was still in wonderful spirits that day on the phone, saying she just needed something to help with her cough. The following weeks were a blur of medical specialists, scans, and emotions, not unlike that October season four years earlier. She fought for days on end, with Gabe traveling back and forth between Tennessee and Virginia and communicating medical updates between medical staff and family. In what would be his final visit with her (though he didn't realize it at the time), Gabe told Darlene I was writing a book on resilience. She broke into a big smile, winked, and gave a thumbs-up as the machines pumped oxygen into her lungs.

Two days later, visiting rights were suspended due to yet another COVID-19 spike in the area, and it was the first time in fifty-three years that she couldn't be with Melvin, the love of her life. She was without access to her children or grandchildren. There, alone in her room for eight days, her body began to shut down.

Darlene was a picture of resilience in the twenty-seven years I knew her. She was diagnosed with diabetes fourteen years earlier. She survived cancer for four years. She fought COVID until the end, and through all of it, she was the one comforting everyone else. The night before she passed, she called our family from her hospital bed, a nurse holding the phone to her ear so she could hear us. Darlene told us she was ready to be with Jesus. Her spirit strong, her body failing, she knew it was time to go home. "I'm at peace and ready to move into eternity," she said, and she reminded us that "to be away from the body" is to be "at home with the Lord" (2 Corinthians 5:8). She told us she would have a new body and every tear would be wiped away.

Because we couldn't get there in time, we pulled together the family for a final FaceTime call. It was our chance to say our final goodbyes. With her husband by her side and our son Pierce present in the room (he goes to college in Lynchburg, Virginia, and was able to get there in time), she rallied. None of us were ready for it, but she was the steady one, and we drew strength from her resolve and peace. It was a celebration of life while she was still alive, while her husband of many decades gently held her hand. We told stories, shared memories, and cried, and toward the end, Gabe asked her if she had any parting words for her children and grandchildren. She pulled the oxygen mask off her face and, straining through every word, uttered the most profound words anyone could speak on their deathbed.

"Stay . . . close . . . to . . . God . . . and . . . in . . . his . . . Word . . . because . . . the . . . truth . . . brings . . . freedom. . . . And . . . if . . . you . . . stray . . . you . . . will . . . never . . . be . . . free."

Within minutes, she was welcomed home by her Savior.

I sat with Darlene's final charge for the remainder of that day, repeating her words in my head. How many times had I been tempted to stray when plans didn't go the way I wanted them to, when I was faced with those crushing, unexpected U-turn moments in life? Regarding these life-altering moments, I eventually accepted them and chose to trust because there was simply no other way. The *everyday* moments? Those were harder for me. I had grown accustomed to my chronic response of frustration when everyday circumstances didn't go my way. I had become oddly comfortable with the low-grade bondage of living life overwhelmed. This is where the enemy took ground, and the slow and subtle striving caused me to stray. And the straying unveiled a sneaky truth: I wasn't as resilient as I would have liked to believe I am.

Darlene's words snapped me awake.

She didn't buy into the narrative that many would wish to thrust on her—that her final years should be reclusive and self-focused. She continued to show up, stay creative, live generously, and always add an encouraging word to any conversation. She taught me that freedom is a mindset. She believed that circumstances are not bondage. She discovered a great freedom even in a body in decline.

What Is the Truth That Sets Free?

Living as a slave to circumstances locks us in mental, emotional, and spiritual bondage. It becomes impossible to find resilience. Jesus taught that when we renew our minds and live in the truth of the Scriptures, we break free: "If you abide in my word, you are truly my disciples, and you will know the truth, and the truth will set you free" (John 8:31–32 ESV).

Simply put, *abiding* means spending time with Jesus, seeking to understand everything Scripture says. It means orienting our lives around these truths, whether they're Jesus' specific words, the wisdom from the books of Ecclesiastes and Proverbs, or the teachings of Paul. When we encounter God's Word and do what it says, we become free (see James 1:25).

You may struggle with this idea because you're not sure you believe the Bible is true or believe what it says. I only share my experience and invite you to engage it for yourself. When I meditate on Scripture, I see life differently. I have a clear-eyed perspective on what is valuable and what is not. I'm less tempted by distractions and can more quickly see through empty promises that have no real substance. I'm less prone to buy into a human definition of freedom.

The prophet Ezekiel describes "eating" the words of Scripture and finding them "as sweet as honey" in his mouth (Ezekiel 3:3). The author of Hebrews says, "The word of God is alive and active. Sharper than any double-edged sword, it penetrates even to dividing soul and spirit, joints and marrow; it judges the thoughts and attitudes of the heart" (Hebrews 4:12). We learn the truth by reading, studying, and understanding God's Word as it pertains to all of life. Not only is it penetrating when it comes to our own lives, but it enables us to discern what is true in our world's epic battle between good and evil.

I'm pressing in here, because in a society that is content to think we each have different truths and they can all be valid, we may be consumed by indifference—even burned-out when it comes to knowing where truth resides. I'm confident you'll never be disappointed in pursuing truth through the lens of God's words to us in Scripture. You won't be swayed by someone embellishing the truth of God's Word with clever gimmicks or fancy platforms or using Scripture to manipulate you. Let me be clear: God isn't in that. Any Scripture used to elevate someone else or to increase your bondage is misused because God's Word brings us freedom.

Darlene had no doubt about her purpose on this earth. The Word was truth to her, which played out each morning as she received it in faith. It stood the test of an entire lifetime, offering hope. It shaped her confidence. It made her strong in death. It gave her resilience.

When she gave her final charge, this was exactly what she wanted us to remember above anything else. Now that you have read this chapter, I hope her resilience based on her hunger for God's Word will encourage you in the days ahead.

We gathered to honor Darlene's life just a few days after her passing. We didn't grieve as those who have no hope; we grieved as people who miss their hero of the faith, a matriarch who passed the baton to her children. We are inspired to live and love the way she did—graciously, joyfully, faithfully, contentedly. With true, faith-inspired resilience.

If you're locked in bondage, believing that your circumstances define you, shift the narrative. Embrace the Scriptures as the truth that sets you free. Experience resilience that comes from fully trusting, believing, and living into God's truth. Darlene did, and it made all the difference.

REFLECTIONS ON RESILIENCE

1. What circumstances have you experienced that made you feel bitter or angry toward God? There is nothing in your life that hasn't been sifted through his hands. Does this statement bring comfort or frustration? Why?

2. I use Scripture as my guide to know what is true. Where have you found guidance to better understand what is true? Does it feel like a reliable, unchanging source?

3. One hundred percent of us will experience physical death at some point in the future. Imagine for a moment a final charge you'd want to leave with those you love. What would it be?

RULE THREE

EMBRACE
ADVERSITY

TRAIN WITH RESISTANCE

We live in an age of "easy everything." We're used to quick and convenient entertainment, fast food, simple navigation, immediate online connection. The more difficult we find things to be, the less likely we are to sustain them. Like water running downhill, we take the easiest path to avoid resistance. It's normal; it's human.

In the first two rules for strengthening resilience, we learned to name the pain and shift the narrative. If we're going to *grow* in resilience, we also must learn to accept and embrace the adversity that makes us more resilient.

What if adversity is a gift?

When we encounter adversity, we face a challenge that requires a decision. Will we run and hide, or will we embrace and overcome? Adversity must be met with an opposite and more powerful reaction. Instead of avoiding it, we must confront it.

Resilience is a muscle developed through responding to adversity in the right ways. Just as physical exercise increases our body's capacity to handle and off-load stress, emotional and spiritual exercise do as well. In this section, I analogize resilience to a muscle, showing how it can only be built through the application of certain training rules:

Treat anxiety as a friend.

Train with resistance.

Grow incrementally.

We become stronger, more resilient people when we face our challenges with a hopeful outlook. Let's commit to doing the countercultural thing and embrace adversity together.

CHAPTER TEN

TREAT ANXIETY AS A FRIEND

CHAPTER TEN

TREAT ANXIETY AS A FRIEND

You gain strength, courage and confidence by every
experience in which you really stop to look fear in the face.
You are able to say to yourself, "I have lived through this
horror. I can take the next thing that comes along." You
must do the thing you think you cannot do.

ELEANOR ROOSEVELT

It was an eventful October weekend in Chicago, and my friend
Angela and I scurried to our flight. Angela joins me sometimes
when I speak, so she was used to the check-in routine: hurried
precheck, speedwalking with only our carry-on baggage, boarding
just before the gate closed, collapsing into our seats to catch our
breath.

When this all began a decade ago, traveling to speak felt awkward
because public speaking was awkward. I fumbled over notes and
outlines onstage, sometimes struggling to connect with the audi-
ence. That situation changed one weekend when, in my hurried

state, I left my laptop on a plane as I ran to make a connecting flight. As my anxiety began to rise without the security of an outline, I remembered God's generous reassurance to Jeremiah, who dismissed God's call by telling him, "I do not know how to speak; I am too young." God's response: "I have put my words in your mouth" (Jeremiah 1:6, 9). I recalled how this sentiment is echoed throughout the Scriptures. God told Moses he would provide the words for him to speak to Pharaoh (see Exodus 4:12). In Psalm 81:10, the Lord told the psalmist, "Open wide your mouth and I will fill it."

That weekend, I spoke three times without notes, and God did for me exactly what he told the prophet, patriarch, and psalmist he'd do for them: He put words in my mouth. This has been my method ever since. I memorize the loose outline, mark the passages I'll teach, and let the Holy Spirit take it from there. When I'm finished, there's a fullness, and yet there's also a sense of being poured out—meaning, by the time I rush to board my return flight home, I collapse into my seat. My spirit is full, but I'm physically exhausted and weak. This happens each time before takeoff, the letdown full and fast.

This October weekend was no different. When I crashed in my seat after a full weekend, I felt full but spent, dozing off during the first leg of the flight. After touching down, I slogged through the airport toward my connection and repeated the pattern on our second flight. Taking my seat in the back of the plane, I slipped my AirPods in and relaxed the only way I know how after a weekend of sensory overload—soft music and a book. I was so immersed when we landed that it took a few minutes before I finally looked up to realize we'd been sitting on the runway for a while with no movement. Angela informed me we would be there for another thirty minutes before we'd arrive at the gate to deplane.

I weighed her words, and my muscle memory set in. This was how my first panic attack happened twelve years ago—back of the plane, fear of being trapped, unable to exit. It had been years since I'd had a panic attack on a plane, but because the brain can't tell time, my trauma sent me right back to that initial moment of panic disorder all those years ago.

Within seconds, I felt acute triggers consume my entire body. My heart rate accelerated into the upper 160s, and I began to grip Angela's hand. I immediately looked at the ground and began to do deep, slow breathing, whispering "Jesus" repeatedly under my breath. There was nothing else I could do but steady my breathing through the duration of the panic attack.

After what seemed like forever but was only eight minutes, my heart rate began to slow down, the trembling subsided, and my breathing regulated. As my body relaxed, silent tears began to fall down my cheeks. I felt a physical release now that the threat was over. The crazy part? We still had to sit in that exact spot for thirty more minutes and I was perfectly fine.

Just eight minutes. The Anxiety and Depression Association of America (ADAA) confirms this: "Although anxiety is often accompanied by physical symptoms, such as a racing heart or knots in your stomach, what differentiates a panic attack from other anxiety symptoms is the intensity and duration of the symptoms. Panic attacks typically reach their peak level of intensity in 10 minutes or less and then begin to subside."[1]

Don't Run from Anxiety; Turn toward It

In the past, I always tried to remove myself from situations of panic, feeling a compulsion to run or escape. I found ways to avoid battling the acute terror of a panic attack, mostly through my attempts at limited exposure, exit strategies, and breathing techniques. Yet this time I didn't have the option to hop off the plane quickly but had to allow the panic attack to roll through my body. To my surprise, it didn't take me out. I learned something profound that day. The attack itself isn't the bully; it's *the fear and shame I feel during the attack* that make me avoid circumstances that threaten it.

It's important to note that my panic disorder thirteen years ago was rooted in claustrophobia. That's why panic attacks were so frequent when I lived in New York City, when I was surrounded by planes, trains, elevators, subways, and crowds. I lived in a city with limited personal space, where eight million people crowd into the span of eleven miles. That's also why my panic subsided once I left there, with some exceptions that still tempt me to avoid exposure. Yet halfway through our time in New York, I was able to confront and reduce the impact of this claustrophobia through small and regulated methods of *exposure* to places that instigated panic.

It took great care to retrain my brain with the safety of others nearby. Gabe and the kids joined me each day on elevators once we moved downtown to the seventh floor of our Tribeca apartment. Using resilience techniques others taught me—wearing earbuds filled with worship, reading the Scriptures, practicing regulated breathing, losing myself in books—I boarded planes each week to teach about God's power to rescue us from harm.

I also kept symptoms at bay through a deep sense of meaning (we'll talk more about this in the next section), by creating beauty, and by sharing with others through writing and teaching. Pain becomes purpose if you let it. These factors were critical to developing resilience when struggling with anxiety and panic.

Most importantly, I didn't avoid the places that trigger my panic. I turned toward them. Research suggests this is what we must do. When we face our pain and discomfort, we experience less of it. When we focus our thinking, a form of meditation, we display decreased activity in the part of the brain involved in the *registration* of pain and increased activity in the areas involved in the *regulation* of pain.

WHEN WE FACE OUR PAIN AND DISCOMFORT,
WE EXPERIENCE LESS OF IT.

Ed Halliwell, mindfulness author and teacher, writes,

> When gently turning towards pain, people report that they experience less of it, and their resistance usually decreases. They may not get so caught up in the negative stories and evasive reactions that tend to accompany pain but do nothing to stop it (and, indeed, may increase the mind's perception of it). This may be why people with chronic conditions have reported reductions in pain after training in mindfulness, even though they still suffer from the illness.

Halliwell continues,

Sometimes our experience is painful and difficult. And there may be little or nothing we can do about the arising of the pain or difficulty. In these cases, we may be able to work with what's happening skillfully by exploring our relationship to it. Most of us have a habitual pattern of turning away from problems or trying to get rid of unpleasant events. Unfortunately, this often seems to increase our sense of stress, because if pain is already present, you can't get rid of it by trying to run away from it. In mindfulness practice we gently experiment with reversing this habit by turning gently towards difficult experiences that come up in our meditation.[2]

On a Personal Note

Before we move on, it's important to address two things I've been asked countless times over the past decade. First, I've never taken medication for anxiety or panic. This was my personal decision, not a judgment toward anyone who does. I wanted to see if my brain could overcome through my faith and regulated techniques. So far it has. Again, I'm not against anyone taking what they need to cope and function in their everyday life.

Second, I'd like to address the root of my panic attacks. For anyone who has experienced such attacks over a long period in their lives, there's a strong chance they've explored the root in therapy. I have several hunches as to what may have caused my panic, most notably the day I became a mother twenty-two years ago.

At thirty-nine weeks, we discovered my amniotic fluid was gone (it had leaked slowly the third trimester). Cade was only four pounds and his heart rate had plummeted into the sixties. The medical team immediately prepped me for emergency surgery, offering me *two* different epidurals within twenty minutes. As the doctor tugged Cade out of my body, anesthesia filled my lungs and I began to slur my words. I remember telling the nurse, "I'm dyyyyyyying." Cade was experiencing failure to thrive, and all eyes were locked on him. I couldn't take a breath and tried not to black out. It all turned out okay, with oxygen and urgent care. I didn't hold Cade for twenty-four hours and couldn't walk for two days until the numbness wore off.

Before each panic attack, I feel trapped and powerless. When I explored this with my therapist, she asked, "What makes being trapped and powerless so terrifying?" Her question triggered my anxiety and pulled me back to my fear of dying on the table that day. Bringing life into the world is costly for everyone; my version just came with some side effects. For whatever reason, those side effects have followed me over the years. Faith has helped me overcome feelings of panic and anxiety by turning my attention away from fear and toward God.

There are plenty of places we can focus our attention when we're plagued by fear, anxiety, or panic, but as Christ followers, we are urged to follow the examples in Scripture. God tells us to meditate on his Word, and research shows how this rewires our brain. This is where science and faith collide.

In preparation for taking God's people into the promised land, God told Joshua, "Keep this Book of the Law always on your lips; meditate on it day and night, so that you may be careful to do everything written in it. Then you will be prosperous and successful" (Joshua 1:8).

The psalmists meditated on the Lord day and night too.

> My eyes stay open through the watches of the night,
>> that I may meditate on your promises.
>>> (Psalm 119:148)

> May these words of my mouth and this meditation of
>> my heart
>> be pleasing in your sight,
>> LORD, my Rock and my Redeemer. (Psalm 19:14)

> My mouth will speak words of wisdom;
>> the meditation of my heart will give you
>>> understanding. (Psalm 49:3)

> I remember the days of long ago;
>> I meditate on all your works
>> and consider what your hands have done.
>>> (Psalm 143:5)

Meditate versus Medicate

MEDITATE THROUGH IT INSTEAD OF
MEDICATE THROUGH IT.

Still to this day, I'm learning how to turn into the pain, to *meditate* through it instead of *medicate* through it. For me medicating looks like coping mechanisms of avoidance and distraction. This doesn't mean I obsess about the pain or camp out in it, but I do pay attention to it. I've learned pain (even the pain of anxiety) is my friend, a barometer that nudges and reveals when all is not well.

It asks me to take a closer look at my life—at my choices, actions, and motivations—and investigate what might need to change. Pain also affirms my dependence on Jesus, showing how his gift of peace leaves my heart tender, full of gratitude and love. I'm drawn back to his heart by meditating on Scripture and praying bold prayers.

In pressing into the pain, I've learned to listen to my body, to pay attention to physical symptoms of stress. For years my breathing quickened when I opened my calendar on my laptop. One time Gabe sat beside me and said, "You're doing that breathing thing again," and he was right.

I took inventory, using Toyota's founder Sakichi Toyoda's "Five Whys" technique to get to the root, the real cause, of the problem.[3] First, I defined the problem. "I display physical anxiety when I look at my calendar." Then I asked "Why?" five times to get to the root.

Why does my calendar cause anxiety?

Because I always overschedule with little margin.

Why do I overschedule?

Because I need to accomplish things in an efficient manner.

Why do I need to accomplish things quickly?

Because there's so much to do and not enough time to do it.

Why am I motivated to do all these things?

Because I want to live a life of significance.

Why do I need to be significant?

Because I believe my worth depends on it.

You can see where this goes. A question of shallow breathing roots in identity and worth. I began to meditate on the truths of Scripture. I was a daughter of God, loved just as I was. There was no accomplishment, nothing I could do, that would make me any more worthy. And meditating on that truth, I decided that I could cut back and free up my calendar. That freedom would help alleviate some of the anxiety, some of the tension.

The older I get, the more comfortable I am with what I call "50 percent Rebekah." This ultimately means I "produce" half as much in my late forties as I did in my early forties. I have no aspirations to build a large organization or travel one hundred days a year. I'm comfortable with phrases like "I can't commit to that." I say no a lot more than yes. I create margin for things that fill me up when I'm empty. Now I breathe easier when I consider my calendar.

What Anxiety Can You Press Into?

There's much to learn from pressing into the pain and asking why. Through pressing in, we come to realize that our fear, pain, and anxiety have something to teach us. They drive us toward God and ask us to meditate on his truths. They reveal areas where we have not yet surrendered our lives. They expose places where we need greater resilience.

> *In what areas of your life are fear and anxiety always present?*

> *What does God's Word say about your particular struggle?*

> *How can you lighten the weight of fear and anxiety or overcome them altogether?*

> *What counselor or friend can help you develop strategies for dealing with pain?*

No matter what your anxiety is, invite God into it. As you do, you will experience greater levels of freedom and build a more resilient life.

REFLECTIONS ON RESILIENCE

1. Name the areas of fear or anxiety in your life. Don't rush it. Do your best to name them all.

2. Ask "five whys" for one of those areas. See what it reveals as you press into the pain.

3. Are there any practical shifts you can make from what you learned, like the lesson I learned to refuse to overload my calendar? Write down three or four decisions that can keep the anxiety or fear at bay.

TRAIN WITH RESISTANCE

TRAIN WITH RESISTANCE

*Even when all is known, the care of a man is not yet
complete, because eating alone will not keep a man
well; he must also take exercise. For food and exercise,
while possessing opposite qualities, yet work together to
produce health.*

HIPPOCRATES

Golf is a passion for Gabe. For me, not so much. But twenty-five years into marriage, with three of our four kids grown, new margin brought new perspective. I love beauty, nature, and exercise—and whenever I can engage in all three with my husband, it's a yes. Two years in, I golf whenever Gabe asks.

I'm not an "eighteen holes" kind of girl, but with some helpful coaching from our friend Ben, a PGA Tour player, and Julie, who may as well be on tour, I hit the ball farther and straighter each round. Though the game of golf can be stressful, it has been a fun surprise to see how much Gabe and I enjoy a couple of hours on the course at dawn, to delight in something beyond work and children. My confidence grows when I experience the benefits of playing this peculiar game. It has become a sweet respite from the cares of this world—that is, until this particular Friday morning.

We were walking off the number seven green, and Gabe calmly said, "I need to tell you something I've been nervous to talk to you about." I leaned in. Anytime your husband goes to a vulnerable place, it's a welcome conversation. He went on. "I don't want to scare you, but for the past month, I've been experiencing a weird pain in the upper left area of my chest each time I take a deep breath. I don't know what it is. I thought I may have stretched a muscle, but now I'm concerned it could have something to do with my heart."

I took a slow, deep breath, keeping my reaction in check, and said, "I'm sure it's nothing big. It's probably just anxiety. You've been carrying a lot since your mother's passing, and sometimes that's how it feels for me—a tightening of the chest."

He replied, "I know what anxiety feels like, and that's not what this is. I think I need to see a doctor and make sure it's not something more serious. It scares me to think of all the possibilities."

I don't remember the next two holes, but that day marked what would become a transformation in our life. Truth be told, I had a hunch something was wrong too. In the months leading up to this, Gabe had experienced more than a few physical ailments. From lower back stiffness and joint pain to foot tendonitis and flaring eczema, the list of maladies mounted. With age, we expect to experience a few setbacks. This seemed different.

Upon returning home, Gabe scheduled his first appointment, which led to another, then another. He went through a battery of tests and then more tests based on the result of the first tests. Slowly, clues came in. His blood work showed extremely high cholesterol, triglycerides, and even calcium present in the widow-maker artery. His gallbladder contained gallstones and his insulin numbers bordered on prediabetic. The mystery was being solved, though not to our liking. Gabe was not only experiencing chest pain; his body was screaming at him, *It's high time to take your physical health seriously!*

Our Bodies Tell the Truth

The fifth decade of life is when a loss of physical strength becomes most obvious. In the book *Younger Next Year*, Chris Crowley and Henry Lodge tell us that biological decline begins to accelerate at age fifty as our bodies naturally break down. Yet studies show that 70 percent of the effects of aging are optional.[1] This means while our bodies naturally decline, we have a choice to counterattack through diet and exercise, a form of resistance training. While we have no idea when our days will be done, we *can* outsmart our biology, at least to some degree. Our genes and predetermined DNA have their limitations, but if we take our health seriously, we can make our bodies more resilient.

Physical and mental decline accelerate when we get comfortable and static. It's usually unintentional, a result of mild pains, but we move our bodies less and less as we age. We buy single-story homes, take the elevator instead of the stairs, go on fewer adventures, and moderate our risks. We play it safe, which feels *far* more comfortable, but ease paves the way toward decline. Comfort doesn't provide the body the resistance we need to build resilience.

Though we can't stop decline and death, we can live resilient, healthy lives beyond the current norms. As it relates to our physical health in building resilient lives, we get to decide: How much resistance training are we willing to do?

Training with Resistance

If anxiety is your friend, resistance is your new best friend! You need it. I need it. We don't grow without it. There's only one problem. We've been conditioned our entire lives to avoid the resistance that comes with hard things.

Modern technology has eased the burden of many daily activities that create resistance. Whether plowing a field, constructing a home, milling wheat, or baling hay, for most of human history, resistance was built into the daily chores of life. Now we see resistance as something to avoid because it brings pain.

Even the word *resistance* conjures up bad feelings—not only in the physical realm, but also in the emotional and relational realms. None of us want to experience resistance in relationships, whether marriage, family, business, or friendships. It's normal to intuitively take the path of *least* resistance. However, in building a life of resilience, especially in the categories of our physical and mental endurance, resistance is not the enemy; resistance is our *ally*.

Our son Pierce took this seriously when lockdowns set in. Home from school and with the option to watch Netflix or doomscroll media outlets all day, he set a different intention—he was going to get in shape. Day after day, we would find him maxing out pushups, dumbbell squats, chair dips; doing HIIT workouts; and pressing anything he could find that gave him a little resistance. It didn't take long. Within weeks, his body took on a new form, and months later, his body had been transformed.

Years later, resistance training is part of his everyday college life routine. Pierce has grown in clarity around his calling, confidence around his gifting—a true joy for family and friends to see. He has helped encourage others in their resistance training journeys too. He has been passionate about music since he wrote his first song at age eight and has now broadened his passions to include health in nutrition and exercise science.

Many of us—athletes and nonathletes alike—use resistance training to improve our health and resilience. The principle behind modern resistance training comes from Dr. Thomas DeLorme's work on progressive loading in the 1950s. DeLorme was the first to suggest a routine consisting of three sets of a ten-repetition exercise, where each set would become progressively more resistant. He believed it was better "to restore muscle strength and then build endurance through low resistance, high-repetition exercise rather than develop endurance in atrophied, weakened muscle."[2]

It's hard to imagine a gym today that doesn't provide some form of resistance. Most have dumbbells, barbells, kettlebells, resistance training machines, stationary and spin bikes, rowers, and high-incline treadmills to create the necessary resistance to build strength. If you don't go to a gym, countless online sites provide resources that use body weight to build strength with natural resistance.[3] When we train with resistance, our bodies become more resilient.

What's true of the physical body is also true of the spiritual body.

The apostle Paul understood that humans build resilience through physical training, and he used this analogy for our spiritual lives as well:

> Do you not know that in a race all the runners run, but only one gets the prize? Run in such a way as to get the prize. Everyone who competes in the games goes into strict training. They do it to get a crown that will not last, but we do it to get a crown that will last forever. Therefore I do not run like someone running aimlessly; I do not fight like a boxer beating the air. No, I strike a blow to my body and make it my slave so that after I have preached to others, I myself will not be disqualified for the prize. (1 Corinthians 9:24–27)

I love how Paul calls it "aimless" to train without intention or to box by beating the air. He uses this metaphor to instruct the young church that resistance is our friend, the fuel for growth and resilience. This is true in both the physical and spiritual sense. He wrote, "I strike a blow to my body and make it my slave." Paul is clear-minded about the important role resistance training plays in overcoming our natural desires. He trains his mind and body to submit to his will to stay resilient when temptation comes.

Training to Resist

In God's beautiful design of the human body, he infused strength of mind as the driver of everything else. Ever wonder how it's possible for someone to walk on burning-hot coals and feel no pain? Our minds were meant to control our bodies, not the other way around. When our appetites are in charge, we respond with instinct and craving instead of with discipline for the greater outcome. This is why we overdo things—whether eating, drinking, sleeping, or engaging in screen time.

Jesus admonishes his disciples to pray even as he acknowledges a natural principle: "The spirit is willing, but the flesh is weak" (Matthew 26:41). We are wired to take the easiest path, to eat what's in front of us, to say yes to the temptation. If there's one thing America excels at, it's providing us with *many* culinary temptations. To resist, we must prepare mentally, emotionally, and physically. Even while in the wilderness, Jesus said no to bread during a forty-day fast. He demonstrated that he cared more about spiritual resilience (i.e., overcoming) than he did about any bodily appetite. He was not like the person spoken of in Proverbs 25:28: "Like a city whose walls are broken through is a person who lacks self-control." Instead, Jesus was the perfect model of the way spiritual resistance leads to spiritual resilience.

Father's Day

This past Father's Day, we gathered around the breakfast table for our annual moment to honor Gabe. I made my favorite farm-fresh frittata and blueberry crisp. It is one of our favorite traditions, where we share a special meal and speak life over the person we are celebrating.

That morning, each child shared how they had taken notice of Gabe's transformation. Pierce commented that he was impressed by the way Gabe was now challenging him physically, a new experience in his late-teen years. Pierce also mentioned how he enjoyed their latest songwriting collaborations, something they'd done long ago, now resurrected as Gabe came to life in so many ways.

Kennedy smiled as she recounted how much fun she was having during their morning workouts. Three months prior, Gabe and Kennedy joined a local gym that combines resistance training and group cardio fitness. They're having a blast and getting fit in the process. She shared how much she loved growing together, working hard, and seeing the results.

I can't deny the transformation either. My husband of more than twenty-five years bounced back into peak physical shape. He now weighs less than when we were married. More importantly, he's healthier and stronger than when we first met.

After we finished, Gabe responded, "These last six months have been life-altering. Earlier this year, I caught a glimpse of being physically debilitated, worn-out, unable to keep up basic responsibilities to sustain a home and family. If I didn't change something, from food and diet to my physical and mental routines, I wouldn't be able to show up for you guys."

With tears in his eyes, he expressed gratitude. "Thank you for supporting, loving, and encouraging me to become the best father I can be. I've felt energy and clarity, more present with each of you than I have been for a long time. I've taken my health responsibility seriously, to be strong and fit as long as I'm able. I love you."

Training with resistance is easy to see in the physical realm, but of course that's what we're doing when we lean into adversity in other ways as well. While this chapter demonstrates how embracing adversity through *diet and exercise* can create a more resilient body, chapter 10 showed how embracing adversity through *confronting anxiety* creates a more resilient faith. In the next chapter, we'll discuss how embracing adversity through *practice and repetition* creates a more resilient mind.

REFLECTIONS ON RESILIENCE

1. Examine your physical, mental, and spiritual life. List any areas where you're experiencing breakdown.

2. List ways you opt for seeking comfort instead of training with resistance.

3. Determine separate plans to engage in resistance training for your mind, body, and spirit. Write those plans in your journal and implement them over the next few weeks.

GROW
INCREMENTALLY

GROW INCREMENTALLY

You can do almost anything if you are willing to clarify your commitments and make incremental investments over time to achieve them.

MICHAEL HYATT

When we first met Joy at age five, she cried silent tears. If she fell and skinned her knee, she ran from the room and hid, gasped for air, and tried hard to be quiet. She wanted to be invisible and wouldn't seek outside comfort. If we ate together as a family and turned our attention from her to someone else, she began a pretend conversation with an imaginary friend in front of us, mimicking yet ignoring us. If there was an argument between her older siblings or she felt any tension between Gabe and me, she addressed that same imaginary friend with stern gibberish, shaking her finger and raising her voice.

Joy's reactions arose from her insecurity around attachment, revealing the work we needed to do, first in ourselves and then with her.

I began to read books on attachment, the trauma of abuse and neglect, and the way it sets a trajectory of insecure relationships for the rest of our lives. These discoveries were alarming and urgent. In the book *What Happened to You?* I came across these words:

> A dismissive, disengaged interaction is not building the foundation for a loving person. On the contrary, it's building the foundation for an emotionally hungry, needy person who will long for belonging but won't have the neurobiological capability to really find what they need. Dismissive caregiving can lead to an unquenchable thirst for love. You cannot love if you have not been loved.[1]

I was convinced. While Joy's caregiving might have been disengaged or dismissive in her earliest years, if we were going to help Joy recover attachment, we couldn't dismiss or ignore her now. We'd need to show her just how committed we were, in the hope that her responses would gradually shift.

At first it all felt so daunting. How would we begin to tell Joy a different story about herself, not just with words, but more importantly with our actions? Even if we told her a different story, could we autocorrect the formation of her first five years, helping her know she'd never be rejected or abandoned? Could she grow in security and attachment? I was determined to find out.

The Secret to Healing the Brain

Let's start with the first year of our lives. If we are born healthy, we arrive in this world hungry for attachment. We look into the eyes of our mother, father, or caregiver, waiting for them to make eye contact and engage back. This is because we intrinsically believe we matter and are hardwired for connection. If we are ignored, we use our fight-or-flight response and begin to cry. If over time our parents or caregivers don't respond to our tears—or when they do, they are irritated or angry—we shut down and eventually dissociate. This response is innate from our earliest days. When we are powerless to change our distress, we descend into our internal world as a means for survival.

Our earliest experiences affect our brains in profound ways. Neurologist and researcher Dr. Bruce Perry writes:

> While a very young child may not understand the words used in language, they do sense the nonverbal parts of communication, like tone of voice. They can feel the tension and hostility in angry speech, and the exhaustion and despair of depressed language. And because the brain is growing so rapidly in the first years of life and creating thousands upon thousands of associations about how the world works, these early experiences have more impact on the infant and young child.[2]

The most common form of neglect affecting development is "fragmented, patternless caregiving."[3] If we have been raised in a household or community characterized by unpredictability, chaos, or ongoing threat, we very likely have ended up with altered stress-response systems. Even when there's no chaos or threat, we can still have the reactivity that comes with patternless caregiving.[4]

As I write this chapter, we're celebrating the fifteen-year anniversary of the iPhone, and since its advent, we've all been impacted by fragmented, patternless caregiving. We place these devices in our children's hands, particularly when we need a break or a nap. We give our children addictive apps, and they create bonds with their phones instead of with real-life people in the real-life world. The result? A digital revolution with an addictive device has changed the way we think and behave.

————

A DIGITAL REVOLUTION WITH AN ADDICTIVE DEVICE HAS CHANGED THE WAY WE THINK AND BEHAVE.

————

Reflecting on the issue of addictive devices raises the question, "Can we heal our brains and create healthier mental conditions for our children?" The good news is that if we are consistent, predictable, and nurturing, we *can* repair our thinking. The stress-response systems can become resilient.[5] This can come about because of our brains' potential to heal.

We Can Rewire Our Brains

Two millimeters per day. That is the average growth of an injured neuron that is in the process of healing.[6] The first time I read these words, I was intrigued. How does trauma injure the neurons in our brain? And how does growth heal them? Historically we've understood that the brain develops most rapidly in childhood, but in the past twenty years, we've found out that the brain has the potential to continue to grow and develop for the entirety of our lives, particularly for those who are willing to put in the effort of rewiring our brains through lifelong growth and learning.

According to scientists, neurogenesis is our brain's ability to grow entirely new neurons, even in adulthood. Just as amazing is the promise of neuroplasticity—the brain's ability to rewire and form new connections. This field of neuroscience focuses on the brain's ability to adapt and learn, based on our environment. Neuropsychologist Celeste Campbell writes, "From the time the brain begins to develop in utero until the day we die, the connections among the cells in our brains reorganize in response to our changing needs."[7]

In short, we have the power to change.

While many of us experience anxiety and may even believe change isn't possible, we have the chance to start mapping new connections. Clinician Ian Cleary writes, "It is not enough to just stop anxiety in any given moment which is often people's focus. The anxiety wiring is still there and waiting to be triggered." He says we must create *new wiring of what we want to achieve* to compete with the old wiring of trauma. "Without this," Cleary says, "we loop endlessly in anxiety with no neural pathway to take us forward."[8]

When it comes to ending our cycles of negative thinking, anxiety, depression, fear, and the like, neuroplasticity is our friend. We can turn our attention toward creating new habits, rhythms, mental images, and intentional focus. We can rewire our brains.

This is wonderful news! We now have an opportunity to declare a fundamental shift in the lifelong trajectory of trauma. It is possible to transform dysfunctional patterns of thinking and behaving into new mindsets, new memories, new skills, and new abilities. As a result, we become better able to respond to adversity in our past and our future. We can become people who are able "to bounce back from setbacks and adversity—to be resilient."[9] It begins with incremental growth through the daily practice of healing rhythms.

How we invest our time matters. The research on neuroplasticity shows that our "day-to-day behaviors can have measurable effects on brain structure and function" and can be key to healing from psychiatric disorders.[10]

This is why I wrote *Rhythms of Renewal*. In that book, I write:

> Through study and experience, I came to understand four rhythms that help us replace stress and anxiety with life-giving peace and purpose. They help us nurture and sustain lasting emotional health. These rhythms aren't complicated—Rest, Restore, Connect, and Create—and they're words I first wrote under the heading "Rhythms of Renewal" the summer I found my own freedom. However, these rhythms do take practice. Practical acts like fasting from media (Rest), exercising (Restore), sharing a laugh (Connect), or recovering an old talent (Create) can help us break the anxiety-inducing cycles of the world around us and bring balance to our otherwise hectic lives. They can help us cultivate the spiritual and mental space needed to allow God to bring us through complacency and fear and into freedom.

> When you consider it, these four rhythms make some sense. The first two—Rest and Restore—are "input rhythms," rhythms that allow the peace of Jesus to fill us. The latter two rhythms—Connect and Create—are "output rhythms," rhythms that pull us out of our own heads and help us engage with the world around us. It's the input of Christ's peace that allowed me to pour out that peace, and when I abide in that input-and-output flow, I don't struggle so much with anxiety. In fact, I find healing and wholeness.[11]

Forming the daily habits and rhythms that keep us in a healthy place is a game changer for rewiring our brains. Making sure our inputs allow us to rest and restore in the healthiest of ways primes our mind and body for the outputs of connecting and creating. Building a resilient life requires both—the daily habits of incremental growth and the developmental mastery of new skills.

Practice, Practice, Practice

I contemplated how we could help Joy feel secure and attached, ways we might be able to help her repair parts of her injured brain that were making her feel most anxious. After much research, we decided to work with what she was learning at school, with more intentional time educating her at home. She progressed quickly in her English by singing educational songs that expanded her vocabulary. She was growing in her conversational skills too. She had shown a remarkable capacity for growing in her motor skills and was building with blocks, putting puzzles together, coloring, drawing, and making beautiful things out of Play-Doh—all the things one would learn in kindergarten and first grade.

I shared with a friend about how quickly Joy was learning, and she told me about a program that helped kids with Down syndrome learn how to read. After doing some research, I saw why the program was so effective. Every session was done in *rhythm*!

The structure required reading at a rapid pace through three or four short handmade paper books, approximately thirty minutes a day, five days a week. It seemed like something we could do, so Joy and I dove in. For weeks we sat on the floor together, starting each session with a squirt of focus spray (lavender spritz) over our heads and saying together, "I am focused!" Then we began with rhythmic movement, which usually involved bouncing a ball back and forth while we recited the alphabet or counted to twenty. Sometimes I offered a category like "animals" or "food," and we threw a beanbag back and forth, spontaneously naming an item in whatever category we decided when it was our turn. This sped up Joy's motor and mental processing, as she needed to think of another animal before she threw the beanbag back to me. Each activity strengthened her ability to focus.

After this kind of active focus, I introduced a new book, saying and circling the words, asking Joy to say and circle the same words after me. We kept pace, repeating each other in rhythm. Time passed quickly, and when we completed our books, she picked a "Happy Sheet" to complete before the session was over. These fun sheets included cutting, gluing, matching, and coloring together. Before we knew it, time was up! She always left wanting more.

The program aimed to get Joy's brain firing automatically, a little quicker each day. After two weeks, she was saying and circling without me, and by week three she could "read" her "unit one" books without any prompting, showing herself to be well on her way to learning to read. The part I wasn't expecting was that this frequent repetition of my undivided attention created a greater measure of bonding between the two of us. I wasn't distracted during her learning sessions, and sometimes we even invited Cade to join in the fun. There were moments when Joy became the teacher, and I the student. She let me pick my favorite color marker and asked me to repeat after her. For Joy, this was playtime with Mommy, and in doing this, she developed a new depth of attachment, which also increased her confidence in learning to read.

My friend Curt Thompson, whom I referred to in chapter 4, says the key to beginning a new practice is *where we direct our attention*. Everything we do, conscious or not, begins with shifting our focus toward a desired target.[12] I directed my attention to Joy, which motivated her to direct her attention to the handmade books that were helping her read. With each session, her confidence grew. She became happier, more lighthearted, and more engaged in other forms of play—from taking our orders on her cash register and serving up our "food" from her kitchen to snuggling and asking for extra hugs at bedtime. This shared intimacy of focused attention not only developed a life skill of reading but also deepened our attachment on the other side of her trauma. She started to say things like, "Scare me," when she encountered something that made her nervous, or "Hug Mommy" with her arms raised when she needed emotional support. Her pretend episodes almost faded. We were approaching breakthrough through the incremental growth of rhythmic practice.

Through Joy, I've seen how connection and bonding create security and attachment. Through my own experience, I've seen controlled exposure to elevators and planes help me overcome a fear of tight spaces. Through neuroplasticity, I've seen how our brains can rewire, allowing us to become healthier and more whole.

What areas of your life require incremental growth for resilience? The good news is that we are not locked into our current fears, anxieties, or ways of thinking. The hopeful truth is this: We are not victims of our earliest formation; instead, we can grow, change, and heal. This growth may be slow and incremental, but it fundamentally changes the way we see and respond to the world.

REFLECTIONS ON RESILIENCE

1. Examine the areas of your life where you feel less resilient. Is it in the arena of your health, your marriage, or your economic stability? Make a specific list.

2. What actions can you take to increase your resilience in those areas? Use your imagination and create action steps to implement habits of resilience in those areas.

3. Talk with your spouse, friend, or spiritual advisor and share your action plan for growing incrementally in resilience in the least resilient places of your life.

RULE FOUR

MAKE MEANING

CULTIVATE BEAUTY

To build a resilient life, we first learn to name the pain and shift the narrative. As we embrace adversity, we begin to build the strength necessary for overcoming new challenges with a hopeful outlook. When we live this way, we open ourselves to becoming a creative force, with God at work in our lives. We can begin to partner with him to create meaning in the world around us. This gives us true purpose, allowing us to solidify our resilience.

When God made Adam and Eve and placed them in the garden, he tasked them with creative jobs. Name the animals. Tend to the soil. Be fruitful and increase in number. He gave them tasks that would fill their lives with purpose and meaning. Ultimately, they created a world of order out of chaos.

We live in a society that wrestles with meaning, a phenomenon that some believe has led to increased rates of depression, anxiety, and despair. Clay Routledge, professor of social psychology at North Dakota State University, writes, "As a behavioral scientist who studies basic psychological needs, including the need for meaning, I am convinced that our nation's suicide crisis is in part a crisis of meaninglessness."[1] This sentiment is echoed by scores of psychologists, counselors, and mental health experts—past and present. When we lose our purpose, we lose our reason to live.

If we're going to be resilient people, it's imperative that we become people who make meaning. In this section, we'll see how encountering beauty and making good things can help us cultivate purpose and meaning. Through these practices, we'll become people of greater resilience.

FOLLOW THE LONGING

FOLLOW THE LONGING

True life is recognizing the moment of glory when you're standing smack-dab in it.

TIMOTHY WILLARD

I'll never forget the moment I realized I couldn't see. It was New Year's Eve, just hours before the dawn of 2020. We were at a restaurant celebrating with close friends, the culmination of looking back on all that God had provided in 2019—Joy's arrival in our family, Cade's becoming a legal adult at the ripe age of eighteen, the launch of *Rhythms of Renewal*. In the dimly lit restaurant, I pulled out the menu and realized I couldn't read any of it. It caught me by surprise, so I held it farther away and squinted until I could make out the words. I ordered and continued the merriment with friends with this lingering thought: *Did my Lasik surgically repaired eye stop working after fifteen years without any problems? Will this get worse?*

Upon ringing in the New Year and returning home, I woke up

early the next day and went about my usual morning rhythm—prayer, Scripture, gratitude, and journaling—while the house was silent. When I opened my Bible, I realized it was a little harder to read but pressed on. As I journaled my first entry of 2020, the irony of losing 20/20 vision rang loud and clear.

My vision worsened in the following weeks to the point I could no longer ignore it, so I scheduled an eye exam at the beginning of March. Thankfully, I was able to purchase my first pair of glasses three days before the mandates began. They were stylish enough, I guess—but glasses? I've never been great at accepting help, particularly help that was such an obvious sign of aging.

As I write these words two years later, it occurs to me that while I began to lose the ability to *see* words clearly, I simultaneously began to lose the ability to *recognize* God's goodness all around me. I'm not sure how or when it happened, but at some point my focus shifted from seeing beauty to seeing lack. I noticed what was wrong, what needed editing or fixing, viewing the world through a critical lens. Why did I shift from a glass half full to a glass half empty? When did I begin to notice what my family *wasn't* doing instead of what they were doing?

When I finally confessed my perspective shift to Gabe and my friends, I began to journal about this ceaseless obsessing. What was I longing for? Fame? No. Ease? Maybe. Comfort? Probably. Inspiration? Sure. Peace and contentment? *Ah, yes. That's it.* Here's the odd thing. Instead of digging into my struggle for peace and contentment, I rejected the things that would bring it—slow mornings in Scripture and prayer, slow days with my family, slow walks on the trail behind my house. I wanted to run.

Restless until We Rest

Augustine says it like this: "You are great, Lord, and highly to be praised. . . . You have made us for yourself, and our heart is restless until it rests in you."[1] Throughout my life, I've been restless, longing for something just out of reach, though I couldn't name it. This yearning ebbed and flowed, quelled when the house was full of laughter and song, when the sun rose gold from the front porch, or when I walked in the hushed dusk down our wooded trail. But my longing reared its ugly head when there was conflict in our home, loneliness in community, or lostness in vocation.

Why the chronic hunger for something more? Will it ever change? Why do I have this lust for something—career, freedom, success—that can never be quenched by anything but God?

Longing is the plight of all God's creatures, and I know I'm no different. N. T. Wright speaks of our deep ache as echoes of a voice—primarily in themes of justice, spirituality, relationships, and beauty. It is God himself who is speaking to us, "whispering in our inner ear—someone who cares very much about this present world and our present selves, and who has made us and the world for a purpose which will indeed involve justice, things being put to rights, *ourselves* being put to rights, the world being rescued at last."[2]

When we feel a craving for something missing, what we desire most is the presence of God in our everyday moments when we feel his silence. If the silence lingers longer than we're comfortable with, even days that morph into weeks, we tend to fill that silence with noise, consumption, or adrenaline. Why? Perhaps it's because what we fear most in the silence is that God has rejected us or, worse yet, abandoned us in the waiting. My friend Timothy Willard puts it well:

> From the time of the ancients until now, human beings have longed for the *thing* beyond. It quickens the hearts of all. It echoes with the tremors of the truest and purest essence of life. But our hearts betray us in our quest to possess the object of our desire. Veering from the path of true presence with God, we settle for shallow gratification tied to temporal things.[3]

As a daughter of God, I now grasp that this craving will never change. What we all crave is a holy encounter with God himself. While we won't get the fullness of such an encounter in our present lives, we get to experience a glimpse of it each day to keep us going. For now, that will be enough.

The beautiful promise through all this is that God has never left me. In the Scriptures, Christ promises, "Surely I am with you always, to the very end of the age" (Matthew 28:20). This is true, and yet our finite, childlike, wandering minds tend to forget this promise. For each of us, remembering and recognizing that God is with us and fills our every longing becomes the tricky part. How do we learn to drink from the wellspring of living water, where we are satisfied even when our circumstances don't change? It begins by noticing what we really *want*.

What Do We Want?

When I first engaged the question, "What do I want?" I sat with it for a while. For so long, I didn't feel I had permission to ask what I *really* wanted beyond the daily cadence of my physical life—coffee, deep sleep, a walk with a friend. But in the larger metanarrative of life, I moved from considering my daily needs to thinking about my deepest desires. I started a long list, then stumbled on something by Curt Thompson that echoed with resonance.[4] I'll paraphrase, then riff.

Our hearts, minds, and souls most desperately want to love and be loved by real people in real time and space. Embodied love. True love. My deepest desires need to have color and sound and pulse. We long for biblical justice—for things to be put right—for relationships to be robust, governed by kindness and honesty. We desire deep connection in friendship or with the one we marry and make a life with.

We want to engage in work we find meaningful, work that requires the sort of effort that lets us know we have left a part of ourselves in it, such as writing a book or a legal brief, composing a song, hand-crafting a piece of furniture, or watching your students graduate from high school. We want to enjoy a healthy body here on earth. Firm muscles, strong bones, freedom from heart disease, cancer, knee replacements, and obesity. We want healthy brains too, neurons that connect and grow and heal.

We long for adventure and human creativity that leave us speechless. We want springs, summers, autumns, and winters that live into their fullness. Finally, we want *resilience*, to abide in God with gratitude and wonder. To tend faithfully to creation, to encounter and be encountered by others without exploitation until, in the end, we die well.

Are you crying yet? I am. What a vision of the kingdom of God!

This *is* beauty in every form. Naming my desire for beauty aligned me with the primal call of God. We were made for beauty and made to serve beauty. At creation, we were placed in the perfect setting of beauty, the garden, where we worked with God to name, cultivate, and enjoy nature. What could be more beautiful than that?

The very process of naming my desire for beauty shifted my thinking. It made me slow down, look for beauty in the world around me. It made me less reactive and required me to determine how I wanted to live in intentional and lasting pursuit of the beautiful things that matter in life. It made me stop and notice God at work in the world around me and helped me see just how present he truly was. As a result, his presence made me feel more loved, more valued, and less restless.

Resilient People Encounter Beauty

BEAUTY IS THE ANTIDOTE TO SCARCITY.

Beauty is the antidote to scarcity. When we fear, we see lack. When we recognize beauty, we encounter the divine. God himself draws us close, and we behold him, the author of beauty itself. Everything God creates is beauty, starting with the newborn babe, untarnished by the world. How do we recover the notion that God created us for beauty? We encounter it.

When I realized I was more obsessed with what was broken than with what was beautiful, I made some changes. I took more walks in nature, looking for the God-created beauty all around me. I noticed baby birds singing a chorus in a nest above my head, natural springs with the sound of water gurgling under a rock, and a green tunnel of leaves with a soft, mossy floor where a mama fox protected her young. (I decided to turn around at that point.)

Encountering beauty isn't just about noticing natural beauty in the world around you; it's about noticing the beautiful things God has planted *inside* you and allowing those things to flourish. It's about reclaiming your creativity and seeing how that creativity is a God-given thing. For instance, I started playing piano at age six, and my theory and practice quickly led me into classical music in my elementary years. I loved playing the piano, but over the years, I let that gift go. When I was thirty-six, Gabe bought me a piano on Craigslist. I broke out my well-worn piano books—Bach's Inventions and Sinfonias from 1949 and the Fishers Piano Classic Collection featuring Tchaikovsky and Brahms from 1968. Occasionally, when the house is empty, I'll pull out those books and play from them again. If you happen to be sitting in the room, you may not recognize it as beautiful—I'm a little rusty—but the beauty of that music awakens my heart. Somehow it helps me feel less restless and more connected to God.

Another way I encounter beauty is by revisiting my family history. When I watch old family movies or go through scrapbooks that have been handed down, I'm reminded of countless expressions of beauty. My mom created unique birthday cakes by cutting shapes from a sheet cake into angels, butterflies, race cars, and sailboats. When I turned five, she even baked and decorated a huge Raggedy Ann doll cake for all my friends to share! At Christmas, we ate fudge from the saucepan with a spoon, long before she had a chance to pour it into the pie pan to harden.

Encountering beauty may mean something totally different for you. It may look like sitting on your back porch, watching the birds, picking flowers, or sitting down to paint. It may mean decorating your house or helping a friend with her hair and makeup or doing any number of things. No matter the expression, when you acknowledge your primal need for beauty, you'll be able to *see* again. See the God who created you in beauty and created beauty for you. There, in beauty, you'll encounter the God who never left. What could make you more resilient?

Resilient People Restore Beauty

A life of meaning focuses on restoration, on taking everything back to the original, beautiful intention. In New York City, we rented an apartment in an 1860s row house. While there was fresh paint and a host of new kitchen appliances, the recent renovations stopped there. We killed sixty-two mice within the first two years. The underground boiler room cellar where we did our laundry was overrun by cockroaches. When the heat from our leaky radiators went out one winter, we endured forty-degree temperatures for a week until the landlord remedied the problem.

When we moved to historic Franklin, Tennessee, years later, I wanted to live in a home that was beautiful and also held some deeper meaning. That said, I didn't want to remodel a historic home and deal with all the problems that came with it. Gabe and I determined that while we loved the timeless charm of an old house, we would look at new construction. To our surprise and delight, we stumbled on a *new* house inspired by and modeled after an *old* house, also from the 1860s. From the floor panels, window casings, and trim and molding to the brick flooring of the galley walkways, the architect and builders paid attention to every detail, even sourcing antique lighting in certain rooms from that era. Their vision of a Greek revival farmhouse came to life.

The designers and builders could have simply plopped any old house on the property. But they had a vision for restoring the setting to an original beauty that was historically accurate, with deep meaning for that particular piece of property.

Now that home inspires us. It satisfies our rich longing for beauty and connects us with a time in history when people worked their farms. It reminds us that we need to restore the beauty on our land, just as the architects, designers, and builders of our home restored the beauty of our property. This inspiration connects us to a different time, a time when people cared about beauty as an expression of the divine. It has led us to work hard to bring that kind of beauty to life where we live.

How Meaning Cultivates Resilience

What if our lack of resilience is due to our lack of beauty making? And what if our lack of beauty making is due to our lack of beauty noticing? When I observe my harder seasons, I see I wasn't working with my hands, playing the piano, going on long walks in nature. I was consuming, being distracted, comparing. I stopped sleeping, started stressing, performed for outcomes I never really wanted in the first place. In those moments, I disconnected from my true desires and, more importantly, from God.

Perhaps we long for the way things were, the childhood eagerness to try something new, to create, to discover, to build. I'm not saying our childhoods were without struggle, but they were also tethered to everyday wonder and beauty. There's less strategy. More inspiration. Who doesn't remember being more connected to desire in that beautiful time of their youth?

On this tepid July morning, I almost feel like a little girl again, captured by beauty. In my garden, dewy tomatoes and cucumbers cling to the vine, ready to be added to a pasta salad to take to a friend's potluck in the afternoon. A group of cyclists ride by in tandem—their colorful jerseys, synchronized pedaling, and state-of-the-art bicycles capture my attention. This time, my noticing of the beauty in the world around me prompts action, and I realize I have an opportunity to create beauty of my own today. My bike is in the garage if I'll use it, the piano is in my living room if I'll play it, and the blueberries on the kitchen counter are for a homemade crisp drenched in vanilla ice cream if I'll make it. I can use my hands and feet for beauty.

Beauty begins in the beholding, and the beholding propels action. That action allows us to connect with God if only we'll let it. There our resilience against the drab, dark, depressing world around us strengthens.

Are you restless because you rest . . . less? Do you nitpick everything—or everyone—around you? Are you discontent, obsessive, and anxious? If so, are you making space for beauty? A life of beauty connects you with God, and in that connection, you begin to see the world differently. You see it as a gift, something given to you in love to be loved. In that connection with the God of the universe, you come to see yourself as a creator of beauty with him.

If you want to overcome your compulsions and anxious obsessions, begin to look for beauty in the world around you. As you do, you'll find more joy and fulfillment. You'll find a light to guide you through the darkness. You'll find a rest that the world can't fathom.

REFLECTIONS ON RESILIENCE

1. Do you find yourself restless? How does this restlessness show up in your everyday life?

2. What is your favorite practice for discovering beauty? How often do you make space to engage that practice?

3. Create a daily plan for discovering or engaging beauty over the next week. Throughout the week, record how intentionally engaging beauty made you feel.

CREATE
FLOURISHING
SPACES

CREATE FLOURISHING SPACES

*The places we inhabit matter. They not only serve as the
backdrop of our memories, they actually help form our
memories and contribute to the Joy we experience daily.*

TIMOTHY WILLARD

I love the charred smells of a true wood-burning fireplace. The
perfect, warm glow chasing shadows across the room and the
crackling sounds of baking heat awaken all my senses. During our
first New York City years, we stared at a beautiful, 1860s marble-
hewn fireplace we never could light. We were told by the landlord
it was simply too old to put a fire in, so we let it sit. What a tortur-
ous temptation!

When we bought our home that mimicked an 1860s farmhouse,
there was only one problem. The fireplace was filled with gas logs.
I tried to get used to it—the convenient flick of a knob, a simple
light with no effort needed—but it just wasn't the same.

I asked Gabe if we could burn real wood. It would require more effort and cleanup, for sure, but we felt it was worth the work, so we converted the gas fireplace into a wood-burning one, and it changed the entire atmosphere. Our living room went from comfortable to nostalgic, from modern convenience to old-world charm.

Every few months, Gabe and Pierce split wood and stacked it to ensure we had a supply of seasoned oak for the winter—wood that created the cozy snap, hiss, and pop of crackling fire. We'd commence lighting fires in October, reading a liturgy aloud to mark the first hearthfire of the season,[1] and not let up until late spring. It was a daily ritual, one that came to feel like home.

I've finally begun to appreciate the settledness of home. Maybe it was the youthful energy of my twenties or the moving to multiple apartments and abodes in my thirties that kept me anticipating the next venture out. Something shifted in my forties. I loved being home. I loved gardening, weeding, walking a nearby trail. I loved a cozy fireplace supplied with seasoned wood. Each time I walk through the door, I fall onto our decade-old, blue velvet couch, snuggle up with my little Joy, and breathe a sigh of relief. Home is where my heart lives.

Spaces That Renew

We all need spaces that allow us to be restored. In the bustle of everyday life, our soul needs order. We need a little peace and quiet. For the longest time, home didn't feel like a place I could get that kind of soul rest. Whether it was the nagging sense that I was little more than a short-order chef for my teens or a part-time entertainer, home became a burden. The road, on the other hand, was the place I could get quiet when I went to other cities for work. I'd collect my thoughts on the hotel bed or enjoy a hot shower without interruption. Home carried all the demands and to-dos, and I had never quite figured out how to balance everything well.

So I set out to create spaces that would make room for soul rest so that I could do everyday life with strength and inspiration. The Danish do this best. They even have a word that doesn't exist in the English language—*hygge*, pronounced "hue-gah" or "hoo-gah." *Hygge* is the feeling of quiet comfort through cozy surroundings that invoke contentment or well-being. Some say it's about making sure people are welcomed right away with something to eat and drink, unless you've invited them to help you cook. Others describe *hygge* as being completely relaxed, alone or with loved ones, as you let go at the end of a busy day of the hectic world around you. No phones or computers are allowed in those magical moments. Sounds dreamy, right?

My favorite description of all? "When you settle in for a *hygge* evening, *everything* you're wearing should be comfortable. There's even a term for your pants that are 'oh-so-comfortable but shouldn't be seen in public: *hyggebukser.*'"[2] We all know we have these pants. We wore them every day during quarantine, even for Zoom calls with a "fancy work shirt" when necessary.

Spaces that renew us don't happen without intention. We can make small efforts to create spaces we can truly rest in, even if little by little. The first place we should do this is where we spend most of our time—our home.

This is how I created mine.

I started by noticing my favorite places to go. What was it about them—color of the walls, cozy seating arrangements, dim lighting—that made me want to sit and read all day? I took note of details from my favorite places—the tastes, the smells, and the sounds that rejuvenated my spirit. Then I got to work.

Inspired to make a commitment to quality over quantity, I looked for items that would last and began to curate furnishings that created the ambiance our family could thrive in. Those things weren't necessarily expensive—a few hand-selected old books over here or an inspiring quote painted by a friend on the wall over there. Gabe contributed a walnut platform turntable and the beginnings of a record collection, while I found table books with photographs that reminded me of my favorite places. A couple of candles placed in the perfect spot, no television in sight, a beautiful heirloom Bible hand-illustrated by our friend Dana. Then the finishing touches of a down pillow, a vintage rug, and a soft blanket to nestle in for relaxing.

If I was going to create a home of true relaxation and flourishing, I'd have to do more than add little touches of beauty here and there; I'd have to set the conditions, which meant figuring out a way to disconnect from the overwhelming high-tech distractions that were keeping me from being fully present in my space. We added a beautiful wooden box that serves as a phone-charging station on our kitchen counter. It's the kind of box you want to use—one that's both beautiful and utilitarian. It allows us to store our phones in a place that keeps them out of sight and out of mind and charges them at the same time.[3] When our phones were in the box, we found ourselves more motivated to do things that rejuvenate us, inspire us, or connect us. Instead of consuming everything—content, products, people—we find true connection with each other, ourselves, and the God of the universe.

Beautiful and cozy spaces are underrated. When we encounter them, we feel the relief. Our bodies crave space to let down. With the frenetic rat race most of us live in, our minds need solace. If we are to remain resilient as we venture into our work, our relationships, and the chaos of each day, we need to make our home base a space of flourishing.

Spaces That Challenge

While our homes should renew and rejuvenate us, resilience is cultivated when we are met with challenge and resistance. This is true of our spaces as well. Just as we choose a gym—a place of literal resistance—to increase our physical resilience, we should engage spaces that challenge us mentally and spiritually as well. Choosing spaces that challenge us is a key building block to a resilient life.

Therapy has opened my eyes to this in recent years. As today's younger generations are plagued with anxiety, depression, self-harm, drug use, and suicidal thoughts, sometimes the most prudent response isn't to medicate or accommodate but to challenge. Wilderness therapy programs have taken off in recent years as a method for desperate parents to help their children get back on track. Instead of sitting for hours in talk therapy, many of these kids find that being in a beautiful yet challenging environment— anywhere from ten to twenty weeks away from home—changes them. They discover they have what it takes to survive, which fills them with confidence. The removal of the comforts, devices, and familiar routines awakens their hearts to all that their lives have to offer and builds the confidence that they can overcome.[4]

You don't have to enroll in a wilderness therapy program. There are many ways to cultivate resilience by placing yourself in the path of new and challenging experiences. When Gabe and I seek adventure, we try to pick experiences we know will be a stretch for us to accomplish successfully. Whether it's going on a complicated hike or biking a downtown urban setting that presents danger at every corner, pushing myself invigorates me. For hundreds of couples, our retreats have taken them out of their comfort zones to ride on the back of a horse or to walk paths that feel more like navigating a high wire above a valley. We've enjoyed marriage intensives that expose us and a small group of people to high-flying ropes courses that force us to work together and reflect on how we can apply our discoveries in our marriage.[5]

Each one of us needs to determine what will stretch us, grow us, build a few new muscles in our minds and bodies, and give us the confidence to stay resilient. It's never the obvious choice because our minds are drawn to ease. Next time you have the chance to go easy or go hard, pick the experience that will challenge and strengthen your resilience.

Spaces That Inspire and Connect

My favorite flourishing spaces are the meaningful ones that bring people together. None of us can walk this road alone. Being resilient isn't about being a solo hero; it has everything to do with having the wisdom to know you need others before you actually do need them. When we gather with common goals, I'm inspired by what is possible.

A few weeks ago, practicing resilience meant hosting a Sunday potluck conversation. Our friend Mike Erwin was coming through town, and Gabe and I wanted to encourage families to imagine sustainable-living, resilient communities in our area. As a former predictive analyst and a leadership and resilience coach, Mike would provide inspiration for everyone navigating an unpredictable future.

When people arrived, it felt a little like a *Little House on the Prairie* picnic. We heated up the barbecue, baked bread, and set out tea and lemonade as everyone arrived with their favorite homemade dish in hand. Before we served the meal, we invited each couple to introduce themselves and share a word about what they were looking forward to that summer. Since a few families were new to town, this event could mark the beginning of new relationships that might make all the difference in whether they felt connected or alone. The introductions took an extra twenty minutes, but they set the stage for an afternoon of authentic conversation.

After dinner, we gathered on our front porch and had a Q and A conversation with Mike. The group felt comfortable asking tough questions that required the wisdom of a man who had served in the military and could envision future scenarios most of us could never imagine. Mike shared that true resilience is built in a community of cooperation, and we left feeling purposeful about implementing ways to continue to grow together. The conversation was much richer because everyone assembled felt connected, even known.

You don't need a military analyst to create a place to inspire. Just look at your friendships and see how you naturally connect. For example, I'd been discipling Cambri, a college sophomore at Vanderbilt, for more than a year. One day we met over coffee. I was prompted to ask if she had any other friends who might like to join us to study Scripture and pray. I also had a mom friend who was discipling some college girls. Within a couple weeks, a group formed, and we began meeting every other week to share, learn, and grow. These young women half my age teach me so much. They are thoughtful, bold, passionate. *They* are the ones who inspire. This space has been one of my favorites this year.

What Kind of Spaces Are You Engaging?

With a little intention, any space can become a resilience-making space. Whether it's a space to recharge and rejuvenate so we can face our everyday challenges, a place of intentional resistance, or a place of connection, spaces create the conditions for us to become better versions of ourselves.

As you examine your own life, ask whether you're creating spaces that enhance your resilience, as well as spaces that enable others to grow in resilience. Creating these kinds of intentional spaces will facilitate our growth and help others see that building a resilient life is possible.

REFLECTIONS ON RESILIENCE

1. What are your favorite spaces in which you can rest and restore, and how can you incorporate the features of those spaces into your home?

2. When was the last time you intentionally put yourself in a challenging situation—one that could remind you that you have the grit to do what it takes? How did you feel after that experience?

3. The next time you gather with friends, how can you be intentional to help connect people at a deeper level? What questions can you ask that will allow people to share thoughts from their hearts that help build connection?

MAKE GOOD THINGS

CHAPTER FIFTEEN

MAKE GOOD THINGS

The only way to change culture is to create more of it.
ANDY CROUCH

Who knew the agrarian life could bring so much meaning? Certainly not me.

I had never thought of milling wheat, baking bread, or planting a garden as a way to find meaning. In my childhood, anything related to working in the kitchen or outdoors was a chore—pure and simple. I remember my dad tending to our backyard most days. We only had a patch of grass between our home and the neighbor's fence, but he thought of it as his citrus grove. From orange trees to lemon and lime trees, he would give his best effort to try to produce a bounty of fruit. A faithful farmer, he would offer us a taste many mornings, reaping what he had sown. Plucking fresh citrus off the trees, proud of what he had partnered with God to create, he was rejuvenated by his handpicked delight. Back then, I never understood why someone would spend so much time trying to grow something when they could just buy it at the store. As I've grown older, the old adage has proven itself true: the apple (or maybe the orange) doesn't fall far from the tree.

When the rapid pace of life hits a pause, I sometimes feel unsettled. It doesn't make logical sense. I'm forced to grapple with where I find meaning. For a decade, I'd experienced great delight in my occupation, in meeting new friends in towns across America. Life operated at a certain hum, with rhythms I had grown accustomed to. I found purpose in helping people contend with their mental health and probe further into their fragility. Together my family had been growing stronger, finding meaning through the pain and trying to make sense out of our chaotic lives. The real test came for all of us when the pandemic hit. There were no distractions, no busyness. Just me, my husband, our kids, and a house.

I used to think that when life slowed down, I would be relieved— more time on my hands, more margin to do the things I love. Yet the silence can sometimes reveal doubt. When I busy myself with endless activity, I avoid deeper questions of meaning, questions like, "Am I distracting myself? Numbing? Avoiding? Living this one life well?" One of my favorite authors, Viktor Frankl, describes this doubt as an "existential vacuum" that manifests primarily through boredom, then leads to distress. He found a pattern to how this doubt would surface throughout the week and coined the phrase "Sunday neurosis" because people became distressed on Sundays when they weren't as busy and had time to contemplate the meaning of their lives.[1]

Many of us experience Frankl's Sunday neurosis in profound ways. The silent pain of not feeling seen can drive us to lead hectic lives—whether we're committed to keep all the plates spinning or simply unable to slow down. For some, it's all we've ever known, patterns that began early in childhood as a way of avoiding pain. Keeping the adrenaline high and the fun nearby, we evade God-given emotions that help us unlock our purpose. Busyness is the saboteur of making meaning. Thankfully, when we ask the deeper questions of God's purpose and allow silence to do its healing work, insight follows. In the words of the folk duo Judah and the Lion, "Healing starts when the unraveling unfolds."[2]

How do we slow ourselves down *and* find meaning at the same time? We make good things. God put this ability to create in our DNA from the beginning. In the Garden of Eden, God instructed Adam and Eve to "be fruitful and multiply and fill the earth and subdue it" (Genesis 1:28 ESV). After the fall of mankind, God reasserted this responsibility, instructing Adam and Eve to "cultivate the ground" (Genesis 3:23 NET). Michael Metzger reminds us that the gospel begins with the cultural mandate—what Dallas Willard called our "human job description."[3] It goes something like this:

Be fruitful—be creative, productive, and effective.

Multiply—have children, for they are a blessing.

Subdue—harness the energy of the natural world.

Cultivate—enrich and improve everything.

This is the motivation to make good things. When we do, our hearts burst with joy because this creative impulse is hardwired into our DNA. Making good things helps us live into the fullness of humanity and find meaning. So why don't we spend more time making good things?

Creating good things takes time.

Creating good things takes intentionality.

Creating good things requires work.

Creating good things takes the long view.

Creating good things requires our full presence.

Creating is costly. It's simpler to resort to busywork, doing, consuming.

It's no wonder the trajectory of the historic rise in depression in Western society follows closely with the rise in consumerism. Few of us truly understand why or how our lives matter, much less how the things we create contribute to God's work in the world. In the confusion and chaos, the daily demands and personal pain, we lose sight of the fact that we've been created to literally *make* a difference. Partnering with God in meaning making fills us with purpose, courage, and meaning. In that way, making good things strengthens our resilience.

Creating Is the Responsibility of the Resilient

When we make good things, we partner with God in his epic plan to bless the world. He doesn't need us, but he *chooses* us! He longs to be with us, inspire us, and renew his world through us. He has given us the ability to imagine and create solutions for the world's problems. Charles Colson and Nancy Pearcey wrote, "As agents of God's common grace, we are called to help sustain and renew his creation, to uphold the created institutions of family and society, to pursue science and scholarship, to create works of art and beauty, and to heal and help those suffering from the results of the Fall."[4]

I write more about my journey of joining God in meaning making in my book *Freefall to Fly*.[5] To sum it up, I found meaning when I began to create things for God's glory, motivated by longing. The most joyous, fulfilled, resilient people in my life have said the same thing. Whether they're teaching children, writing stories, baking bread, creating businesses, running gyms, or throwing dinner parties, those people who are focused on creating good things are full of purpose.

If you're not engaged with God in making good things, you run the risk of falling into the existential vacuum. Making good things doesn't have to be grandiose. It can be as simple as making someone cookies, writing a letter to a friend, or creating a backyard garden. These little things will begin to fill you with purpose and give your day-to-day existence more meaning.

Meaning Increases Mental Health

God designed your mind, body, and soul to make things. Because you are made in God's image, when you create, you are infused with his imagination to set the world right. That's why creating and cultivating does wonders for building your strength of mind and body—the foundation of a resilient life.

Psychologists, neurologists, and everyday people alike know that mental health improves from the simple activity of using our hands, whether by gardening, baking, knitting, sculpting, painting, doing carpentry, reupholstering furniture, or the like. When we work with our hands, we relieve stress and improve neuroplasticity—the brain's ability to adapt.[6] In her book *Lifting Depression*, neuroscientist Kelly Lambert suggests that the key is to find manual tasks that light up our brain's reward centers through cognitive effort, concentration, and the pleasure we get out of the task.[7] The science bears out that the "axis of eye, hand, and brain is a perfect intellectual and emotional 'constellation' which can provide many benefits."[8] Working with our hands releases serotonin and endorphins and reduces our levels of cortisol—the hormone responsible for stress.

To build resilient lives, we should imagine life without our current comfort and convenience. Ask the questions, "How would I fare if all of this went away?" and "What skills do I possess that are valuable in a changing economy?"

Timeless Trades

Rory Groves, author of *Durable Trades*, does us a service by investigating the most resilient vocations that have stood the test of time. He notes a variety of jobs that survived major upheaval in the past and continue to carry a great deal of value today. He lays out the "professions that have proven to be the most durable throughout history, place, governments, economic cycles, invention, and collapse."[9]

As you think about a few of these top historic professions, ask yourself, *If I were forced to provide value to my community in one of these ways, could I?* Could you be a farmer, carpenter, midwife, gardener, painter, cook, brewer, innkeeper, tutor, mason, silversmith, interpreter, author, butcher, counselor, or lawyer? I was only slightly comforted to see that "author" made the list, though I wonder if anyone could find a book these days if online purchasing were to go away, since fewer and fewer brick-and-mortar stores exist! Other timeless trades are barbers, bakers, fishermen, ranchers, schoolteachers, and clergy.

Take a few moments to list the skills you possess that could make you more resilient, both psychologically and economically. If you were to develop more resilient skills in any of these areas, which would be most natural for you, given your talents and time?

The Resilience of Making Things

In addition to being an author, I now consider myself an (amateur) baker and gardener. Two years ago, I was neither. Change forced me to reassess how I was using my hands and whether I'd be able to provide for my family in meaningful ways. In the world of writing and Instagram, my fingers were doing some work, but not the kind that brings fulfillment to the "eye, hand, brain" constellation. In that new season, I found meaning by creating things that made my family more resilient.

I'm grateful for the people who helped along the way. I called Ben and Heather, friends who are some of the greatest hosts I know. Each time our family visits their home, we leave raving about their freshly baked sourdough bread. I wanted to try it, but we have several gluten-intolerant eaters in our family. When I heard the fermentation process of sourdough reduces the side effects of gluten, I was hooked!

Ben and Heather invited me over for a hands-on training session, complete with a tutorial on measuring scales and kneading techniques. At the end, Heather generously gifted me with a "starter." I left her house encouraged, dough in hand. There were a few failures out of the gate. Doughy bread and half-risen batches were part of the learning curve. Now I bake a fresh loaf of bread every few days. Each time I see the kids reach for a slice, I know that this work of my hands has made a difference. I've partnered with God to provide something special for them and decreased my reliance on the grocery store just a bit.

It's not just bread though. This morning I enjoyed pruning our raised-bed garden. Gabe and I established the garden during the early weeks of 2020. It was an opportunity to use our hands in ways that would produce a reward. When we weed our garden or trellis a new cherry tomato or cucumber vine, it's fulfilling to see the resilience that God has built into creation. These little seeds grow and grow. Even in the heat of the summer or when a downpour of rain with high winds cripples a stalk, their ability to rise to the occasion, no matter the circumstance, teaches me that life goes on, even when conditions aren't optimal. This is the way God designed it.

Unlike my father's calling, my path wasn't to pioneer citrus growing in the heart of Tennessee. Instead, I enjoy the fruit of our fig trees. Most summer mornings, I delight in the ritual of pulling a few leaves of basil from the garden to top off a farm-fresh egg on sourdough (don't forget the "everything but the bagel" seasoning). This small act—and the breakfast that goes with it—demonstrates the joy of partnering with God to cultivate expressions of resilience.

We are just beginning to feel the momentum in our journey to make good things, things that nourish us and give us a sense of purpose. When we make good things with an eye toward the future, the meaning we make will outlast our lives and strengthen others. This makes everyone more resilient psychologically, physically, and economically.

How are you partnering with God to make good things? In what ways are those things making you more resilient? If you're still exploring this idea, consider adopting a new practice that cultivates resilience in a chaotic world. If you already have this kind of skill, share it with others, just like Ben and Heather did with me. Teach someone to sew or make bread or plant a garden or do woodworking or . . . whatever! As you do, you'll find joy in knowing that you're making systems that are stronger, more connected, and more resilient.

REFLECTIONS ON RESILIENCE

1. List your "making" skills.

2. Examine your list. Which of these skills do you use on a regular basis? Which need honing?

3. Examine what gets in the way of your practice of making good things. Is it the television, social media, an endless buzzing of activity? Take an inventory, then make a plan to ruthlessly eliminate whatever distracts you from the practice of making things.

RULE FIVE

ENDURE TOGETHER

INVITE OTHERS IN

We were not made for isolation. We were made to be in relationship with God and one another. The entire story of the Bible—from Genesis to Revelation—bears out this reality. Still, our culture is increasingly isolated. Many of us saw this play out over the last few years with the closings of schools, churches, and restaurants. The truth is that we've been increasingly isolated for years. We work virtually, date virtually, even have virtual conversations with friends all day long. This kind of virtual life is both historically anomalous and ultimately unhealthy.

To be truly resilient, we must name the pain, shift the narrative, embrace adversity, and make meaning. These first four rules are more individualistic in nature. The final rule—Rule 5—asks us to be resilient people in a resilient community. Building a resilient life can't be done alone. It requires the intention to come alongside others, embrace diversity, and enjoy the bounty of community.

What does this look like? In *Leadership Is a Relationship*, Mike Erwin and Willys DeVoll write the following:

> A resilient culture means grabbing hands and leaping together, knowing that the leaping will go better because you're not alone. Everyone is encouraged to leap, and it's hard to stay pinned to the ground as neighbors pull your hands skyward. When we're resilient, we jump back into our lives, into situations where we may fail again, into more potential pain. We might be jumping to a beautiful and satisfying new era of our lives, or down into an even deeper, darker well. We jump regardless, and we jump together.[1]

How do we create a community that jumps together? We come together with intention. We work for the good of our neighbor. We . . .

- link arms, join hearts

- build small and strong

- harness the power of we

LINK ARMS, JOIN HEARTS

CHAPTER SIXTEEN

LINK ARMS, JOIN HEARTS

God doesn't intend for you to handle all the pain and stress in your life by yourself. We were wired for each other. We need each other.

RICK WARREN

When the world shut down, we all went home. Holed up with our spouses, kids, even some of our extended relatives, we saw every hidden thing come to the surface and manifest through marital tensions, adolescent rebellions, food and drink addictions, positive and negative coping mechanisms, and anxieties. Plenty of ink has been spilled about these negative revelations of the pandemic lockdowns—articles, essays, tweets, Facebook posts, entire books. Much less was said or written (or TikToked) about the *positive* aspects that surfaced because of the pandemic. For us, those things included the strengthening of our local, embodied community in the city of Franklin, Tennessee.

Six months before the pandemic hit, Gabe sensed a need for deep commitment to the Scriptures and developing friendships among men, so he began a weekly Bible study. Every Tuesday at seven in the morning, thirty men crammed into our cozy downtown Franklin office, each reading a few verses of the assigned Bible passage before discussing the text as a group. It wasn't an accountability group or a specific church-structured small group. It was just an old-fashioned Bible study, which grew through organic invitations from the participants to their friends.

When the lockdown arrived, these weekly studies took to Zoom, in keeping with our local mandates against in-person events. As providence would have it, the group had been working their way through the New Testament, and the onset of the pandemic coincided with their study of the book of Revelation. In private, Gabe admitted he was nervous about tackling this book because he knew he wasn't a New Testament scholar, and apocalyptic literature is notoriously difficult to understand.

Early in Gabe's preparation to teach the text, he read this promise a few words into Revelation: "Blessed is the one who reads aloud the words of this prophecy, and blessed are those who hear it and take to heart what is written in it, because the time is near" (1:3). With a desire to be faithful and trusting the promise that it would indeed be a blessing, Gabe and the men dove in. When you begin reading about the plagues and wars of the end times in the middle of a global pandemic, those words hit a little closer to home.

What began as a desire for the Word in community flourished over the following months. As they gathered in person, those men had fresh fire—a renewed confidence to lead their families and an emboldened conviction to imagine new ways to flourish in a confused society. It was as if the Word became flesh and dwelt among these men communally.

Over the months, I asked several of the men in the group, "What is so compelling that keeps bringing you back each week?" Sure, it was nice to study the Scriptures with friends in the comfort of a small home. A far greater magnetism, a resilient hope, was emerging from the pages of Revelation as the apostle's letters to the seven churches drew them in. They read about the church in Smyrna that stayed faithful through persecution (2:9). They read about the martyrs who hadn't walked away from the faith, even in the face of death (6:9–11). They read about the saints who overcame the enemy through faithfulness to the word of their testimony and the blood of the Lamb (12:11–12). As they read, hope sharpened their minds and fanned the flames of an aligned mission, a mission that would take a persevering community to achieve.

A Gathering Church Is a Growing Church

In the first book about the early church—the book of Acts—we see the connectedness of the first Christians. It was a dangerous time for those followers of Christ. The Jewish leaders saw them as heretics, a crime punishable by stoning. The Romans saw them as revolutionaries and carried out the murder of their leader. Still, even as they faced these existential threats, they didn't retreat into hiding. Luke records this:

> They devoted themselves to the apostles' teaching and to fellowship, to the breaking of bread and to prayer. Everyone was filled with awe at the many wonders and signs performed by the apostles. All the believers were together and had everything in

common. They sold property and possessions to give to anyone who had need. Every day they continued to meet together
in the temple courts. They broke bread in their homes and ate
together with glad and sincere hearts, praising God and enjoying
the favor of all the people. And the Lord added to their number
daily those who were being saved. (Acts 2:42–47)

Despite the threats to their liberty and lives, the first Christians
pursued Christ in the face of persecution. They devoted themselves
to the study of Scriptures, the fellowship of the Lord's Supper, and
prayer. As they became spiritually strengthened, they took inventory of each other's needs and the needs of those around them (the
topic of our next chapter). What was the result? They increased in
solidarity to a cause and to one another. That increase in strength
made them a resilient people, a people able to weather the storms
of persecution that would follow for almost three hundred years.

Right around Easter, I had an idea. Though many churches were
shut down—ours included—I arranged to have a group of people
come together on our front lawn to worship, break bread, and share
in resilient community building. As each family arrived, spreading
blankets throughout the yard, the joy of gathering in the face of
uncertainty was empowering. Though we were starting small, it
was worth a shot, considering the anxiety, fear, and isolation that
were settling in. We set out to explore what a gathering community might look like.

Resilience Grows with Common Commitment

Over these last few years, friends and family members have shared
how sluggish, weary, depressed, or anxious they are. When they

do, I nod and share a bit of my own experience—the times in this unprecedented season of adversity when I've been *all* of those things. It's okay. We're living in a new moment of seemingly unending adversity and social isolation, and it has undeniably influenced our mental health.

The pandemic's timing created a perfect storm. The mental health of people in Western societies was already on the decline at a time when we were forced to isolate even more. For example, before 2019, "just over one in ten adults (11%) reported symptoms consistent with a diagnosable anxiety or depressive disorder. By July 2020, however, that number had skyrocketed to 40%."[1]

I know the adage—"Correlation is not causation." But the link between the pandemic's timing and people's deteriorating mental health is stark, and the negative impact should come as no surprise. However, there have been glimmers of hope during the crisis, specifically within the college student population.

One recent study examined the role community played in building resilience among college students during lockdown. The researchers defined SOC (sense of community) as "a feeling that members have of belonging, a feeling that members matter to one another and to the group, and a shared faith that member needs will be met by their commitment to be together."[2] In their conclusion, they noted this:

> The higher the SOC [sense of community] college students felt, the less they reported feeling stressed. Although the relationship was weak, as SOC increased, disruptions to the daily life of college students also appeared to be reduced. This suggests that SOC could be an important protective factor that may have

the potential to boost college students' ability to cope with the COVID-19 pandemic.[3]

In an article by the American Psychological Association titled "Building Your Resilience," the authors discuss ways to bolster resilience. What's their first recommendation? Build connections with empathetic, understanding, and like-minded people, both in one-on-one settings and in groups.[4] In other words, the APA recognizes that resilient people need the support of other resilient people.

How Crisis Improves Mental Health

Historically, disasters didn't always mean strained mental health; in fact, it was quite the opposite. Social scientist Charles Fritz was among the first to recognize our human response to challenging times as awe-inspiring. His fifteen years of research culminated in his 1961 paper titled "Disasters and Mental Health," in which he summarized 144 studies and 16,000 interviews with those impacted by calamities. These disasters took many forms—earthquakes, epidemics, fires, floods, tornadoes, and hurricanes. He encountered people during their worst moments, their lives upended, completely disrupted with no assurance of what tomorrow would bring.

What he concluded was mind-blowing: *When faced with tragedy and disasters of epic proportions, humanity rises to the occasion.*

Contrary to popular beliefs, "antisocial behaviors, such as aggression toward others and scapegoating, are rare or nonexistent. Instead, most disasters produce a great increase in *social solidarity* among the stricken populace, and this newly created solidarity tends to reduce the incidence of most forms of personal and social pathology."[5]

In times of disaster, people become more unselfish, kind, and caring. They are driven by an urgency to help others. Experiencing disaster awakens the senses and stirs core beliefs about what really matters. In fact, most rescue efforts during a crisis happen as neighbors and friends take immediate action long before professionals arrive. Time and again, this kind of personal agency becomes the bedrock for strengthened mental health and resilience.

The greater the tragedy, the greater the meaning, purpose, and resilience. Fritz concluded, "Disaster-struck societies not only quickly rebound from disaster but often reconstruct and regenerate their social life with added increments of vitality and productivity."[6] Communities not only recover; they become stronger, more livable, more resilient.

This outcome intuitively makes sense. We watched it play out from our apartment in New York City. Only ten years earlier, the Twin Towers of the World Trade Center tragically descended to the ground, wiping out the lives of thousands of people and decimating an entire community. Our children were students at the elementary school where several parents had dropped off their kids and said their last goodbyes on that fateful morning.

A decade later, other than the 9/11 memorial, all visible evidence of those suffering days is gone. An entirely new and bustling community is now built up around it. New restaurants, grocers, retail shops, residential buildings, parks, and museums and memorials fill the grid of the old disaster zone. Life is bursting at the seams, and as we watched the installation of the final panes of glass in the top of the new tower, our community took pride in the realization that this neighborhood was becoming a favorite destination—completely revitalized, stronger than ever. The lesson was clear: resilient people and communities are formed by difficult circumstances.

RESILIENT PEOPLE AND COMMUNITIES ARE FORMED BY DIFFICULT CIRCUMSTANCES.

Cultivating a Holy Imagination for Resilient Community

Gabe and his Bible study group discovered the power of biblical truth and sound psychology—that we are stronger and more resilient when we commit to a common cause with like-minded people. As they studied, prayed, and shared their personal trials and struggles, they came to see just how connected they were. When one had a need—a loss of income from a struggling business, for example—they all chipped in and met the need. When one had a marital struggle, they prayed for this couple. And as they leaned into Christ and community, a new vision emerged: *If this kind of community increased their strength and resilience, maybe they could share it with the local community.* What could sustainable service look like on a local level?

Because they kept up with world news and events and because they were doctors, educators, and businessmen, they already had a glimpse of what would only grow worse eighteen months down the road—shortages; loss of loved ones through death; mandates that, at the very least, paved the way for government overreach; the potential of a society to spin out of control. These men did not embody a posture of despair like others had done; instead, they cultivated a holy imagination for what it could look like to embody gospel hope in their own communities, in a community that helped me understand that resilience isn't simply an individual trait we cultivate.

Maybe you'd like to be part of a group of people committed to form a deeper, richer community. Consider what you might do to forge that kind of community. Don't think of this in terms of starting a huge movement, but rather in terms of building something small. What does that mean? Let's find out.

REFLECTIONS ON RESILIENCE

1. Examine your community. List the people who help lighten your load.

2. What can you do to strengthen your community and make it more resilient?

3. Call at least one person on your list and set up a time to discuss ways to link arms. Imagine together what it might look like to share life together (be specific).

BUILD
SMALL AND
STRONG

BUILD SMALL AND STRONG

Though she be but little, she is fierce.

WILLIAM SHAKESPEARE

I'm fascinated with the Amish way of life. Maybe my fascination came from the horse-drawn carriages I'd see riding along the Illinois highways during childhood summer vacations. Or maybe from their stores, where we'd stop to buy a jar of homemade apple butter to spread on freshly baked biscuits for a snack. Perhaps it was the odd connection I felt to their fashion-backward disposition, since in my conservative upbringing, I grew up wearing culottes instead of shorts. For many reasons, their throwback way of life resonates with me.

I suppose this resonance is understandable. I spent childhood summers escaping the Florida heat by visiting my mom's cousin in Arthur, Illinois, who had married a man who grew up Amish but left the community to marry her. They remained close to his family and farmed in an area adjacent to that Amish community. My mom has the best childhood stories about visiting their farm. The summer before her senior year of high school, she helped her cousin, who was raising young toddlers at the time. The assistance didn't end there. Mom killed, plucked, and processed eighty-three chickens to put in the freezer for winter. She also learned to drive a tractor in a straight line. (I have a photo of me riding that old tractor two decades later.)

Mom also told me about the first barn raising she experienced. All the surrounding farmers showed up bright and early one Saturday morning, with tools and supplies in hand. They worked together from dawn until dusk until the work was done. By the end of the day, the barn was built! Women arrived to load tables with food and drink to celebrate, while children ran around and played. I can't imagine watching a barn go up in a day. What a sense of accomplishment and camaraderie!

The Amish inspire me with their strong bent toward resourcefulness, creativity, and collaboration—an inclination that runs counter to our technologically advanced, modernized world. Their rich, countercultural commitment to resist modern convenience and maintain tradition and valued heritage is no longer commonplace, but their steadfastness pays off during hard times. And while the resilience of the Amish may not feel relatable to your modern circumstances, I believe they have something important to teach us.

Less Is More

In a culture obsessed with size, we've been trained to believe that bigger is better. It's a near-inescapable mentality because it's all we've ever known. We go faster, do more, consume more. But "bigger is better" isn't an old, tried-and-true idea. In fact, it's new.

The twentieth century's economic revolution set new expectations for what Western societies would value. As a result, we started counting and measuring differently. We produced more and consumed more. The wealthy were able to buy newer and more modern conveniences. The more you were able to consume, the higher your status became in society.

In the last couple years, we've become aware of how vulnerable this kind of thinking can make us. Whether it's supply chain issues that impact what we build or the reality that our grocery stores are filled with food from faraway countries, we've come to grasp that "more, more, more" is not sustainable. Perhaps there's another way.

Throughout history, the most resilient communities were small and far more focused on how they could take care of their needs with local resources. They were bands, clans, and tribes who shared land, family ancestry, religion, and agricultural interest. They worked together to ensure their collective survival. In fact, Sebastian Junger reports that "two of the behaviors that set early humans apart were the systematic sharing of food and altruistic group defense."[1] In other words, you knew your community by those you fed and kept alive. Pretty simple calculation.

Size Doesn't Equal Strength

Throughout the Scriptures, we see how the resilience of a community is not dependent on its size. Rather, resilience has to do with cultivating communities of people committed to doing what God asks. We see this in the life of Jesus. He changed the entire world with only a handful of disciples who were committed to doing whatever they were called to do. After Jesus' ascension into heaven, when the disciples were without their leader, they banded together to create a resilient community called the church—a community that still exists today. Jesus doesn't need "big" to be effective or resilient, a truth he demonstrated in his famous parables of the mustard seed and the yeast.

> "The kingdom of heaven is like a mustard seed, which a man took and planted in his field. Though it is the smallest of all seeds, yet when it grows, it is the largest of garden plants and becomes a tree, so that the birds come and perch in its branches."

> He told them still another parable: "The kingdom of heaven is like yeast that a woman took and mixed into about sixty pounds of flour until it worked all through the dough." (Matthew 13:31–33)

God can take the smallest things and use them to change the world. He can make incredibly resilient communities out of small groups of resilient people.

Recently, our Q Ideas organization hosted our annual culture summit. Gabe always invites the most interesting people to share their expertise in a TED-style format, but this year was different in an innovative, backward kind of way. Author Donald Kraybill, an expert on Amish communities, taught us what we could learn from a life lived in intentional community.[2]

Kraybill shared how the Amish put the community first and the individual last—the exact opposite of the way most of us live. They hold the community in the highest regard, placing their family next and themselves last. This upside-down way of viewing their lives prompts them to always think of others. It explains how decisions that appear odd to the rest of us work perfectly well within their tribe. Instead of driving cars or getting licenses—which would immediately begin to widen their footprint and take their people out of the community—they opt for horse-and-buggy transportation and keep everyone close. Instead of telephones in every home, they place one with a time limit in the middle of the community so longer conversations can stay inside the community. They make these kinds of decisions generation by generation, putting the community first so their way of life stays intact for the next.

Not dissimilar from neighborhoods, the Amish have their own way to intentionally create small communities. Districts—or congregations—number between twenty and forty families, adding up to 125 to 150 people who rotate from home to home every other Sunday. They keep the number small to ensure that relationships can form that go beyond surface level. And so if Sara's mother died a few years ago, everyone knows her story and can show compassion and give practical assistance when needed. Or if Michael's brother needs a short-term job in the summer, a neighbor can extend an offer.

This is more than church; it's a group of people who intentionally live life alongside one another. When the congregation outgrows the home they meet in, they split off and form another congregation—always sensitive to staying small. As Kraybill says, "They have a strong feeling that when you move in the direction of bigness, individuals become only a number, only a cog in the machine."

Kraybill recalled a conversation with a carpenter whose family business included only his son. Kraybill asked, "Why don't you grow this into a larger enterprise?" and with a quip of a response, the carpenter replied, "Bigness ruins everything." This adage sums up the Amish way. They function as an extended family committed to making life together work. When they hit an impasse or need a little wisdom, they come together and talk it out to find the best solution.

For most of us, our families are a higher priority than the community. But there is something we can learn from people who view their responsibilities as bigger than just their immediate families. Scripture uses the term "family of believers" (Galatians 6:10; 1 Peter 2:17; 5:9) to describe a group bigger than family that has influence on one another.

We've seen that kind of connectedness play out in our family and among our community of friends. Emily (in her twenties), Kelley (in her thirties), and Abby (in her forties) all speak into my daughter's life, helping to shape her into a woman of God. I'm grateful to speak into their lives too. When there's a need in the community—whether physical, emotional, or financial—we all chip in to help. We're only able to do that because our community is small enough for us to be truly connected. We've deliberately become even more connected, even more committed to the ideal of living small so we can make big impacts in each other's lives.

If you're reading this book, chances are that you're not part of an Amish household. You may not have developed a small community of people (apart from your family) that you'd feed or fight for. You may not have systems in place to take care of needs in community. But if you want to live a truly resilient life, community is a necessity. It helps us get through hard times. It allows for the pooling of resources and gives encouragement in times of chaos.

What might this kind of small and resilient community look like?
How might it function? Let's take a look.

REFLECTIONS ON RESILIENCE

1. Consider the closest twenty people in your life. Do
   you know their history, their needs, their burdens?
   Do they know yours? If they needed your help, would
   they even know that you cared?

2. Reach out to the people you listed, even if it's only one
   couple. See if they'd be willing to join in creating a shared
   community, and then ask what skills or resources each
   would be willing to contribute to the community.

3. Write out your desires and goals, noting the ways you want
   to forge community.

HARNESS THE POWER OF WE

HARNESS THE POWER OF WE

Moral improvement occurs most reliably when the heart is warmed, when we come into contact with people we admire and love and we consciously and unconsciously bend our lives to mimic theirs.

DAVID BROOKS

What is *church*? How do we define it when our definitions change over time and can depend on a number of variables such as the passing of time and the experience of crises? When do we lose track of what it means and how? How do we bring meaning back to the word? I wasn't sure how to define *church* in early 2020, and if truth be told, before the lockdowns began, I didn't even know I would have to revisit the concept of church.

The women had a front-row seat as the men in our circles experienced real life together—studying, praying, and serving each other. Together they were recreating the church of the first Christians. I wanted in, and other wives did as well. So we began our own weekly Bible study. Each Tuesday, we gathered as women—same structure, same vision. We entered inspired and hopeful. Eager and vulnerable, we tended to each other's needs with a simple group text thread.

As we worked together in community, I was reminded of something the ancient apologist Blaise Pascal once wrote about a great wager that everyone must make. He urged his readers to bet on God in this wager, for "if you win you win everything"—truth, happiness, and the good—and "if you lose you lose nothing. Do not hesitate then; wager that he does exist."[1] Investing in community is the same kind of wager. If we win, we win a full and flourishing life, and if we lose, we've made a lot of friends to help us endure the hardship.

We began waking up together—waking to passion and purpose, to conviction, to what it means to be the church. Our awakening propelled us to be the hands and feet of Christ in the world around us. We were being revived one by one, and once we're revived personally, we begin to be revived corporately.

Our community began hosting town hall meetings with local business owners, curating conversations with city leaders, laying groundwork for community gardens, planning schooling alternatives, and organizing medical support for frontline workers. Just as in the book of Acts, numbers were being added to the men's Bible study and community initiatives by the day. The women were activated too, and we looked for ways to serve one another, starting a group text thread to facilitate needs.

Who needs prayer?

Who needs a meal or a care basket because of a loss?

Who needs a ride?

Anyone requiring a doctor recommendation?

Who needs a wedding venue because their previously chosen venue closed its doors?

It wasn't just the text thread. We rolled up our sleeves and got about our work of being the church. We hosted "church" on our front lawn because we couldn't forsake our "meeting together" (Hebrews 10:25). Family blankets took the place of pews. One family led worship from their blanket, with my friend Christy leading the chorus and her husband, Nathan, accompanying with his guitar. Another family read Scripture and led a discussion. Since each family brought their own Communion elements, other families led in the time of Communion and prayer. That afternoon, we were living what N. T. Wright described in his book *Simply Christian*: "The church is first and foremost a *community*, a collection of people who belong to one another because they belong to God, the God we know in and through Jesus."[2]

By early summer, the First Front Lawnist Church of Franklin was on a roll. Not only were we hosting worship gatherings, but on one beautiful May Saturday, we hosted a wedding for Molly and Peter, one of the men in this multigenerational community. Because every venue was shut down, we created our own. The families and several guests gathered—seated in a dozen or so wooden chairs under a canopy of trees, with wind chimes as our backdrop. A path meandered down the slope to a short hop over the stream for the bride's entrance. It was a full Lyons family affair, with Pierce playing guitar, Joy serving as the flower girl, and Gabe and me reading the Scriptures. It was glorious.

Real-life church services brought a breath of fresh air, particularly for our kiddos. The extended isolation was hitting them hard, especially those with differing abilities who were nonverbal. During the many months of not meeting together, events were canceled, including our annual Best Buddies prom. Live events were substituted with online events, which weren't necessarily helpful for everyone, including Cade.

A couple families had seen how much our in-person community lawn gatherings had helped Cade, and they decided to put on the best prom ever for Cade and many friends in our community. The prom took place in a local "party barn" donated for the event—complete with a red-carpet walkway, massive balloon arch, photo booth, and a step and repeat banner photo backdrop. The meal included chicken tenders and sparkling sodas. Cade wore a tuxedo and escorted his date, Kennedy, who wore a floor-length blue silk dress. They danced the night away with more than fifty friends, all of whom were desperate to celebrate together. It was the highlight of their spring.

In our first five years in Franklin, we thought we had been "doing community." We attended church regularly and would often have people in our home for dinner or impromptu parties. In 2020, we learned a different way of *being* a true Christian community. It was the kind of community that depended on one another, not just as some sought-after Christian ideal, but as a genuine mechanism for flourishing. We depended on one another for even our most basic needs—food, fellowship, and even the occasional financial need. We came to realize that resilient lives are not formed in isolation; resilient lives are forged in community.

We Are a Communal People Created by a Communal God

In what became known as his "farewell discourse," Jesus prayed for a unified community, a collective church that was bigger than any one individual:

> "My prayer is not for them alone. I pray also for those who will believe in me through their message, that all of them may be one, Father, just as you are in me and I am in you. May they also be in us so that the world may believe that you have sent me. I have given them the glory that you gave me, that they may be one as we are one—I in them and you in me—so that they may be brought to complete unity. Then the world will know that you sent me and have loved them even as you have loved me." (John 17:20–23)

In the same way that God has inherent interpersonal relationship between the Father, Son, and Holy Spirit, so Jesus prays that we will be image bearers of God in the way we participate in our own community. In the book of Acts, we see the first vision of Jesus' prayer come to fruition when the Holy Spirit is poured out on the people of God and the church comes into existence.

Jesus recognized that the church is made up of individuals who believe in him, but he did not simply pray for "them alone." He prayed for them together—in community. He prayed for our relationship with one another, that we would experience the kind of relationship he has with God the Father—a relationship of complete unity. As we saw in the previous chapter, that prayer for unity came to life in the earliest gatherings of the church. It came to life in our own gatherings too.

What did we find?

In a unified community, we found a more holistic version of resilience. We became an unshakable community that helped meet one another's needs. This began to spread to our broader community among friends in other cities.

We are far more resilient as a whole community than as self-sufficient individuals. The difference is staggering. When the Holy Spirit unites his people, the church, through consistent commitment to the Scriptures, prayer, and one another, a holistic resilience emerges that becomes unshakable both in the individual and in the group. It's an irrepressible force that creates a more resilient world.

We Were Made to Need One Another

We live in an individualistic society, one that teaches us that *self-sufficiency* is resilience. We were not made to resist adversity alone; we were made to have our needs met in community, which is why resilience isn't cultivated in a vacuum. In fact, the Centers for Disease Control and Prevention recognizes the role of community in building resilience: "Community health resilience measures the ability of people, businesses, governments, nonprofit groups, and faith-based organizations to *work together* to create systems that can withstand, adapt to, and recover from a public health emergency."[3]

Research shows that a strong support system or resilient community during times of adversity allows us to bounce back. Many of us don't need a research study to tell us what we already know. Why is community so important in building resilience?

True community reminds you of who you really are. A community of like-minded people calls forth the character and integrity they believe you embody. They hold you accountable so that your inside matches your outside, your private life matches your public life. It reminds you that you're stronger than you think, you're braver than you think, you're more loved than you think. Christ-centered community encourages you to grow in connection to Christ too, which makes you infinitely more resilient. That "calling forth," particularly when done in love and consistent community, creates true belonging. It gives you permission to be known and to know others. When you belong, you are beloved and your gifts are seen and celebrated—and when your gifts are seen and celebrated, they can be used.

Resilient People Create Resilient Communities

In those months of lockdown, I came to appreciate the simple things again. I kept asking myself, *What do we really need in life?* Food? Shelter? Clothing? Yes, yes, yes. But I realized those things were only part of the equation. I needed people, relationships, community—that was the real prize. I needed relationships with people who were willing to encourage me, to offer a helping hand and to receive one as well. I needed people of prayer, of the Scriptures, of worship. I needed the church to be the church. I needed to be the church with my friends too. Because together we were more resilient. Together we were able to create more resilient structures for others too.

There's nothing more magnificent than belonging to a resilient people who roll up their sleeves and do the work they were called to do—the kind of people who surround the parents of a child who is contemplating suicide, who show up in the driveway at midnight when a husband is threatening divorce, who counsel (and confess their own temptations) when a couple is considering walking away from each other. This is the exact kind of community we've forged over the last handful of years, a community that works together for the good of the whole.

This kind of living saved me from spiraling into fear and anxiety, even when I didn't realize I needed saving. I had been pouring myself out for more than seven years, both locally and across the country. I attended conferences and spoke at churches, and all of this was some version of community, I guess. But as I poured into all these other communities instead of forging my own local community of mutual dependency, my spiritual reservoir began to dry up. I started to feel like I had little to offer. It was the beginning of burnout. Timed as it was with the onset of the pandemic, my situation couldn't have been more dangerous.

Burnout sets in when we try to give from an empty place, and empty places are often created when we're in isolation. As most of us know, isolation is possible even when we're surrounded by people. In my case, I was moving from service to service, place to place, people to people, all without the meaningful, mutual, holistic community we were created to enjoy. I found I'd lost passion for corporate expressions of faith—particularly virtual ones such as online church.

When I directed my gaze to my real-life community, things began to change. Through the Bible study Gabe started and the resulting study group of women I became a part of, we experienced a community reminiscent of the church in Acts—a people who "were together and had everything in common" (Acts 2:44). Through this experience of community, I remembered Christ the cornerstone once again, and he rehabilitated my marriage, my parenting, my real-world friendships, and my broader community. In other words, resilience isn't found in the power of me; resilience is formed in the power of *we*.

CHRIST-CENTERED COMMUNITY REMINDED ME WHO I REALLY WAS AND CALLED FORTH CHARACTER AND INTEGRITY IN ME AND OTHERS.

Christ-centered community reminded me who I really was and called forth character and integrity in me and others. Christ-centered community encouraged each of us to use our gifts for the good of the group and to press into our purpose and calling. As a result, we became an Acts 2 community, the by-product of seeking the Word together, which cultivated a unity pointing to the kingdom where every need is expressed and people respond to meet it. It was that community that made us a truly resilient people.

In the last two chapters, you've considered the people who could form your community. You've examined your skills, passions, and goals. Are you ready to invite others into resilient community? Don't wait for the next crisis. Start now to create a resilient community that cares for one another.

REFLECTIONS ON RESILIENCE

Make this your ongoing reflection:

- Create a community journal that tracks your progress as a community.
- Keep a log of your successes and failures.
- Keep a list of events and birthdays.
- Write down new dreams and initiatives you've tackled as a community.
- Note prayer requests and miracles you've prayed for and waited for until God moved.
- Record generational blessings—the children in your community you prayed for and the way God used those prayers to display his power.
- Make a record you can return to at the end of each year and ultimately pass down through the years.

CONCLUSION

CONCLUSION

AWAKE

Wake up, sleeper,
*   rise from the dead,*
*   and Christ will shine on you.*

EPHESIANS 5:14

G abe surprised me in May with a birthday trip to New York City, our first visit back in three years. We arrived for a long weekend without kids or agenda—our only goal being to be active and visit our favorite spots. After fulfilling our activity goal—sixteen miles by bike and fifty thousand steps by foot—we took a trip down memory lane.

We walked past our old apartment and couldn't help but laugh at our first memory of the place. When we arrived in 2010, our moving truck was ticketed for illegal parking—twice. Though I had measured all of our furniture before moving in to make sure it would fit in our tiny floor plan, I hadn't accounted for the height of the stairwell turns. (Remember Ross yelling, "Pivot!" in that famous episode of *Friends*?) Half of our furniture never made it upstairs. I remember slumping onto the floor in tears that night, wondering what kind of mistake we'd made. Not willing to throw in the towel quickly, Gabe responded, "This is the worst day you'll ever experience in the city." Always the eternal optimist—be careful what you promise, Gabe.

Later, we walked past 63rd and Lexington and the F Train entrance, where, in my mid-thirties, I boarded the train to head to Parsons School of Design week after week. Our youngest had marched off to kindergarten, and it was the first time in a decade that my days were free. Parsons was my attempt to remember the "Rebekah *before* kids," to round out my identity and purpose outside the home. While I loved my classroom experience, it became clear that fashion and interior design would remain a hobby, not become a vocation. God had a different plan. He would rescue me from panic attacks a year later, give me a story I couldn't shut up about, and help me begin to write books on faith and mental health. He would reveal purpose in the pain I had experienced in that city.

We continued on our journey down memory lane, crossing Park Avenue at 64th Street and heading toward Central Park as I flashed back to my oldest child, Cade, sitting down in the middle of six lanes of traffic, refusing to get up. I remembered using all the strength I could muster to scoot him to the median, where we collapsed and cried about an unknown future while unfazed, uncaring drivers whizzed by. We were only two months in, and we'd had no idea how this new city would impact Cade. But it took the demands of New York City to force us to kneel down to his level, navigate the pressures he faced, and help him find his footing on new ground.

Over a celebratory dinner at Tavern on the Green—I always get their birthday cake dessert, even when it's not my birthday—we recounted the grace that God gave us to *choose* challenge to reshape our entire lives. We had fought to love a place that was costly, which made our love for the city so much more valuable. We laughed over some memories. We recalled some of the more difficult memories too, like the night I experienced my lowest of lows, the darkest night of the soul that eventually became my night of rescue. In the city, God met me and healed the chronic terror that gripped my soul.

Looking back, I can see that we were just starry-eyed thirtysomethings who wanted more from life. Before we moved, we felt as if the script had already been written. We felt stuck. If we stayed put in Atlanta, we'd be left wanting. So we put all the chips on the table, cashed out of everything we knew, and took a risk on New York City.

That risk changed our lives. It brought hidden pain to the surface, pain we had to name. It taught us to trust God's truth, to shift narratives in accordance with his Word. It taught us to embrace adversity and to allow it to strengthen us little by little. We learned that all of it—our pain, our confession, our adversity—gave us new purpose and meaning. We learned also that we needed a community of committed friends to make it in the city. The city taught us the lessons of resilience, even if we didn't know it at the time.

We weren't the only ones who learned resilience though. Our kids became more resilient. They learned to play in concrete jungles instead of on grassy playgrounds. They grew close to friends with a shared faith and made friends with no faith at all. Their little hearts grew in new surroundings, forcing them to engage in all manner of conversations with a world that no longer saw God as a reliable option. They became compassionate toward people with stories they couldn't quite comprehend, including Louis, our neighbor who spent his days at 61st and 3rd Avenue and his nights in a homeless shelter. He became a family friend and our kids learned that not everyone has a warm, comfortable place to lay their head. They continued to visit him after we moved downtown. After Louis became ill and died, they grieved his loss.

When I think back to our time in New York, I'm filled with gratitude, and that night with Gabe in the city, I felt grateful to be reliving all those moments.

If I'm being honest, our life today feels more comfortable, less exhausting—and that's partially by design. On our trip to the city, I was reminded that I need challenge in my life to continue growing. Resting on my laurels at any point is a recipe for future disappointment. Engaging challenges, after all, makes me stronger and more resilient.

At the end of our weekend down memory lane, we ducked into the last of the Sunday services at the church we attended when we lived uptown. It was the fourth service of the day, and the room was humming. My old friend Suzy got up to teach on grief, and I sat in the back row, taking it all in. In some ways nothing had changed, and yet everything had changed. Like the rest of the world, this community of believers had survived for more than a year without in-person worship. Their city had endured the highest rates of mortality in the nation. They'd witnessed chaos and riots in the streets. And yet their joyful worship was so palpable that I couldn't hold back tears.

After Suzy finished teaching, no one wanted to leave. As they sang softly, people circled the room to pray for anyone who asked. There was a surrender in their survival, a resting in the one who sustained them, an even greater passion on the other side of adversity.

I wondered what was so different about that room. How did they seem more joyous and hopeful on the other side of trial? How had they flourished instead of languished, like so many of the rest of us in the past few years?

I couldn't say it in the moment, but I know the truth. They banded together and helped each other weather the storm. They had become a resilient community. And now, having come through adversity, they knew future storms wouldn't rattle them so much. In fact, future storms might even give them an opportunity to love deeper, grow stronger, and serve more passionately.

In the days after visiting that church service, we found that God got loud again. He reminded me that he had never rested during the pandemic or whatever trial each of us personally experienced over the past few years. Instead, he leaned in. He held us when we couldn't feel him, whispered when we couldn't hear him, and stayed by our side when we couldn't see him. He had led me into deeper resilience, first individually, then with my family, then with my community. And he'd done it all through adversity.

Adversity Brings Opportunity

To everything there is a season, friends. I believe God is allowing the church to grow in strength, hope, and meaning. I've had to ask myself:

Am I willing to grow in resilience through community?

Am I ready to push myself, be bold, risk security?

Am I willing to foster hope in the world?

With deep conviction, I want to say that I am. At least I hope I am, and maybe that's a start. I'm ready to wake up. I'm ready for my courage to return. I don't want to be lulled back to sleep. I'm ready to rise from the slumber of fear, shame, and anxiety. I'm also ready to rise from the slumber of success, affluence, and boredom. I'm ready to be smaller but stronger. I'm ready for my kids (and their kids, once they have kids) to be drawn to the heart of God. I'm ready to see God's love poured out on the world in fresh ways through his resilient community—the church. This will be a marathon, not a sprint, friends. We're going to need some resilience.

Here's the point: Adversity awakens. It awakens us from our comfort and numbing. It awakens us to what we are capable of. It awakens us to what's worth fighting for. It awakens us to what it means to follow Christ.

ADVERSITY AWAKENS.

As a church, we've been through dark days. We'll go through dark days again. With all the unique challenges our world is experiencing, our cultural moment is unlike anything past generations have experienced. While I pray for more peace, for more health and unity, I know there are no guarantees. In fact, trend lines point to more complicated and less comfortable times, seasons that will require true resilience.

No matter what our world throws at us, no matter how dark or desperate the cultural landscape, we can move into it with purpose, meaning, and resilience. With God's help, adversity is meant to make us stronger. Through that Spirit-born strength, we become a living model of Christ's power to the world around us.

Maybe you've been following Jesus for a while and you need to be reminded of this power that is available to you. After a few years of living in the comforts of Franklin, Tennessee, I know I did. Through adversity, I was reminded that I was in a battle and I was made to overcome. I was reminded that I was created to be a messenger of the kingdom of God, which will come on earth as it is in heaven. I was reminded that I am more than a conqueror through Christ. Ultimately, I was reminded that the trials of earth not only are passing but also will lead us into greater resilience if we let them.

Resilience is indicative of the Christian life.

———

RESILIENCE IS INDICATIVE OF THE CHRISTIAN LIFE.

———

Maybe as you've read this book, as you've reflected on the last few years, you've realized you haven't been as resilient as you would have liked, that a lack of resilience has kept you from participating with God to advance his kingdom. Take some time to reflect and to ask God to begin to build resilience into your life.

Ask him to help you name the pain and to show you the truth so you can shift the narrative. Ask him to teach you to embrace new adversities so you can grow. Ask him to help you make meaning in a world that needs resilient hope by sharing the good news of the gospel. And look for a community of like-minded people who want to build resilient systems for the glory of God.

Maybe you're not sure about this whole God thing, and you don't know whether he can lead you into resilience. Maybe you didn't grow up with faith, or maybe you walked away from the faith a long time ago. Maybe God took on the face of someone who rejected, abandoned, or abused you, or the church turned a blind eye toward your hurt. If that's the case, I want you to know how sorry I am. You are beautiful. No one should endure this kind of pain.

God is here for you. He wants to lead you into a resilient life that is full of meaning and purpose. Perhaps you can begin with a simple conversation. Can you name your pain? Can you share your anger, sadness, rage, tears, and despair and ask God for peace? See what God does. He is ready to meet you if you are willing. He says, "Here I am! I stand at the door and knock. If anyone hears my voice and opens the door, I will come in and eat with that person, and they with me" (Revelation 3:20). Are you willing to invite God in?

Maybe you aren't ready to take that step and are more comfortable testing the waters. Take that approach and try incorporating these rules of resilience into your life and see whether God is true to his promise: "Never will I leave you; never will I forsake you" (Hebrews 13:5). I'm confident he will be faithful.

For all of us, it's time to awaken to resilience. The adversity never stops. How we prepare and build our lives to withstand the challenges that confront us will make the difference. When we incorporate the rules of resilience—name the pain, shift the narrative, embrace adversity, make meaning, and endure together—into our lives, we'll find ourselves ready for the next storm, the next trial, the next hardship.

We'll find ourselves with strengthened legs, able to walk through the most difficult times. We'll discover a depth of relationship, one that allows us to work as one church, together with God, to bring his love and light to a dark world. We'll awaken to true and holy resilience.

ACKNOWLEDGMENTS

To Gabe, my forever love: What a joy it is to be your wife for decades, to partner in everything we put our hands to, to raise and launch children with you! You've shown me endless grace and belief when I lacked it and offered me the courage to press on. We've weathered adversity in countless ways and are closer for it. Thank you for being my rock, always holding space for new dreams to emerge.

To Cade, Pierce, Kennedy, and Joy: Loving you is my most sacred call. Each year, motherhood teaches me more about God's lavish grace—whether I see it in Cade's sweet smile, Pierce's tenacious passion, Kennedy's loyal and inspiring faith, or Joy's endearing trust. Even when I feel ill-equipped, God shows me how to nurture your hearts, to seek forgiveness when necessary, and to see his kingdom impact through your lives. I love cheering you on!

To my mom, my father-in-law, and all our siblings: Watching you overcome adversity with the loss of Poppy and Meeme is beautiful. There's no journey quite like ushering someone from death on earth to life in heaven, but I count it an honor to watch you grieve, heal, and become stronger and braver, with lives full of meaning. Thank you for modeling resilience in such tangible ways.

To local girlfriends who dug deep on this resilience journey: From a Tuesday morning tribe that held nothing back as we pored over Scriptures and experienced new levels of healing, to new and old friends who moved from around the country to share burdens of life and loss, each of you tethers suffering to celebration and laughter. I can't thank you enough for this fullness, accountability, and love. You are a vision of what it means to endure together.

To the *Rhythms for Life* community that has journeyed alongside me this last decade: From my writing and speaking to my podcasts and retreats, you challenge me to keep growing, inspire me to keep sharing, and remind me that each of our stories makes a difference. I pray this message of resilience empowers your family, friends, and community with the utmost of joy. Special thanks to Abby Coutant for supporting all this from the beginning and to Angela Cross for being my road warrior and friend.

To my agent Meredith Brock, who championed this message when it was just one phrase—"how adversity awakens the human heart": This idea was enough to dream into and watch come to life. To Seth Haines, my editor and longtime friend: Thank you for listening, tweaking, and ideating till the end. To Tessa Baker, who managed more than I could imagine: You are a gift! To Hannah Crosby, who took my call to ask about your beautiful artwork; to Riley Moody, who made it into a cover; to Aaron Campbell, who is meticulous with typography design: You know how much this means to me. You make words beautiful. Thank you!

To my comrades at Zondervan—Carolyn McCready, Sara Riemersma, Webb Younce, Paul Fisher, Katie Painter, Devin Duke,

Dirk Buursma, Denise Froehlich, and Amanda Halash—and also to publicist Katie Bell of EPIC: You've each worked endless hours to help craft something beautiful and place it into the world, the church, the families, and communities that will find comfort and strength through resilience. In all my years as an author, I'm still amazed and energized by your enthusiasm. It's contagious.

NOTES

Chapter 1: An Era of Overwhelm

1. See "Frequently Asked Questions about Ambiguous Loss: What Are the Types of Ambiguous Loss?" Ambiguous Loss, Pioneered by Pauline Boss, www.ambiguousloss.com/about/faq, accessed October 20, 2022.
2. See Charles E. Fritz, "Disasters and Mental Health: Therapeutic Principles Drawn from Disaster Studies," University of Delaware Disaster Research Center (Historical and Comparative Disaster Series #10; 1996), https://udspace.udel.edu/bitstream/handle/19716/1325/HC%2010.pdf, accessed October 29, 2022.
3. "Coping with Stress," Centers for Disease Control and Prevention, www.cdc.gov/mentalhealth/stress-coping/cope-with-stress/index.html, accessed October 22, 2022.

Chapter 2: What Is Resilience, Really?

1. Neil Postman, *Amusing Ourselves to Death: Public Discourse in the Age of Show Business* (1985; repr., New York: Penguin, 2006), xix.
2. "Building Your Resilience," American Psychological Association, January 1, 2012, www.apa.org/topics/resilience/building-your-resilience.
3. "The Tree and the Reed," Fables of Aesop, July 3, 2016, https://fablesofaesop.com/the-tree-and-the-reed.html.
4. Cited in Laurie Goodstein, "Serenity Prayer Skeptic Now Credits Niebuhr," *New York Times*, November 27, 2009, www.nytimes.com/2009/11/28/us/28prayer.html.
5. Douglas McKelvey, "Liturgies of Sorrow and Lament: For the Death of a Dream," in *Every Moment Holy*, vol. 1 (Nashville: Rabbit Room, 2021), 232, italics added. Used with permission of the author.

Rule 1: Name the Pain

1. Seth Haines, *The Book of Waking Up: Experiencing the Divine Love That Reorders a Life* (Grand Rapids: Zondervan, 2020), 90.

Chapter 4: The Weight of Shame

1. See Curt Thompson, *The Soul of Shame: Retelling the Stories We Believe about Ourselves* (Downers Grove, IL: IVP, 2015), 62–66.
2. Thompson, *Soul of Shame*, 67, italics added.

Chapter 5: Invite Others In

1. See Elizabeth A. Segal, "Five Ways Empathy Is Good for Your Health," *Psychology Today*, December 17, 2018, www.psychologytoday .com/us/blog/social-empathy/201812/five-ways-empathy-is-good -your-health.
2. Segal, "Five Ways Empathy Is Good for Your Health."
3. See Rebekah Lyons, *Rhythms of Renewal: Trading Stress and Anxiety for a Life of Peace and Purpose* (Grand Rapids: Zondervan, 2019), 25–32.
4. Sonny Guild, "The Ministry of Presence: A Biblical View," *Leaven* 2, no. 2, https://digitalcommons.pepperdine.edu/leaven/vol2/iss2/3.

Chapter 6: The Rhythm of Confession

1. Quoted in Brian Kolodiejchuk, ed., *Mother Teresa: Come Be My Light: The Private Writings of the "Saint of Calcutta"* (New York: Doubleday, 2007), 33.
2. Frederick Buechner, *Telling Secrets* (San Francisco: HarperSanFrancisco, 1991), 2–3.
3. Tyler Staton, *Praying Like Monks, Living Like Fools: An Invitation to the Wonder and Mystery of Prayer* (Grand Rapids: Zondervan, 2022), 83.

Chapter 7: Preach to Yourself

1. See Eugene H. Peterson, *A Long Obedience in the Same Direction: Discipleship in an Instant Society*, 2nd ed. (Downers Grove, IL: IVP, 2000).
2. "Free Download: Take Inventory Guide," www.rebekahlyons.com /takeinventory, accessed November 4, 2022.
3. See Jack Wellman, "Where Did Jesus Travel While on Earth?" Patheos, December 17, 2015, www.patheos.com/blogs/christiancrier /2015/12/17/where-did-jesus-travel-while-on-earth.
4. Quoted in Sadie Robertson, "How You Can Be Happier: Practical Tips and Advice / Sadie Robertson Huff and Dr. Daniel Amen,"

WHOA, That's Good podcast, February 23, 2022, www.youtube
.com/watch?v=47oYilrpBNc.

Chapter 8: Retrain Your Brain

1. See Maria Abenes, "Teens in America: How the COVID-19 Pandemic
   Is Shaping the Next Generation," *Psychiatric Times*, November 12, 2021,
   www.psychiatrictimes.com/view/teens-in-america-how-the-covid-19
   -pandemic-is-shaping-the-next-generation.
2. Cited in Ann Pietrangelo, "Left Brain vs. Right Brain: What Does This
   Mean for Me?" Healthline, updated May 9, 2022, www.healthline.com
   /health/left-brain-vs-right-brain, accessed October 22, 2022.
3. Cited in Diana Wells, "Fun Facts about the Brain You Didn't
   Know," Healthline, updated July 6, 2017, www.healthline.com
   /health/fun-facts-about-the-brain, accessed October 22, 2022.
4. René Descartes, *Discourse on the Method* (Chicago: Open Court,
   1910), 35.
5. Napoleon Hill, *Think and Grow Rich* (New York: Penguin, 2005);
   Adam Grant, *Think Again: The Power of Knowing What You Don't
   Know* (New York: Viking, 2021).
6. Jeff Orlowski, dir., *The Social Dilemma* (Boulder, CO: Exposure
   Labs, 2020).

Chapter 10: Treat Anxiety as a Friend

1. "Symptoms: Panic Disorder," Anxiety and Depression Association
   of America, https://adaa.org/understanding-anxiety/panic-disorder
   -agoraphobia/symptoms, accessed November 4, 2022.
2. Ed Halliwell, "The Science and Practice of Staying Present through
   Difficult Times," *Mindful*, July 31, 2019, www.mindful.org
   /science-practice-staying-present-difficult-times.
3. See "5 Whys: The Ultimate Root Cause Analysis Tool," Kanbanize,
   https://kanbanize.com/lean-management/improvement/5-whys
   -analysis-tool, accessed November 4, 2022.

Chapter 11: Train with Resistance

1. See Chris Crowley and Henry Lodge, *Younger Next Year: Live
   Strong, Fit, Sexy, and Smart—Until You're 80 and Beyond* (New York:
   Workman, 2004), 7–8.

2. Cited in William J. Kraemer et al., "Understanding the Science of Resistance Training: An Evolutionary Perspective," *Sports Medicine* 47, no. 12 (December 2017): 2415–35, https://paulogentil.com /pdf/Understanding%20the%20Science%20of%20Resistance%20 Training%20-%20An%20Evolutionary%20Perspective.pdf; see also Jan Todd, Jason Shurley, and Terry Todd, "Science from Strength: Thomas L. DeLorme and the Medical Acceptance of Progressive Resistance Exercise," *Iron Game History* 12 and 13, nos. 1 and 4 (August 2014): 72, https://starkcenter.org/wp-content /uploads/2020/01/IGH2014_08_v12n4_v13n1-Complete.pdf.

3. Resistance exercises are crucial for strengthening the body. See "The Twenty-Five Sacred Exercises," www.workman.com /features/ynyexercise/ynyexercise-sacred-25-cheat-sheet.pdf; see also Chris Crowley and Jennifer Sacheck, *Thinner This Year: A Diet and Exercise Program for Living Strong, Fit, and Sexy* (New York: Workman, 2013).

Chapter 12: Grow Incrementally

1. Bruce D. Perry and Oprah Winfrey, *What Happened to You? Conversations on Trauma, Resilience, and Healing* (New York: Flatiron, 2021), 166.

2. Perry and Winfrey, *What Happened to You?* 32.

3. Perry and Winfrey, *What Happened to You?* 162.

4. See Perry and Winfrey, *What Happened to You?* 61.

5. See Perry and Winfrey, *What Happened to You?* 58.

6. See Curt Thompson, *The Soul of Desire: Discovering the Neuroscience of Longing, Beauty, and Community* (Downers Grove, IL: IVP, 2021), 126.

7. Celeste Campbell, "What Is Neuroplasticity?" BrainLine, February 4, 2009, www.brainline.org/author/celeste-campbell/qa /what-neuroplasticity.

8. Ian Cleary, "Neuroplasticity and Anxiety," IanCleary.com, May 3, 2015, http://iancleary.com/neuroplasticity-and-anxiety.

9. "Neuroplasticity," *Psychology Today*, www.psychologytoday.com /us/basics/neuroplasticity, accessed October 22, 2022.

10. David Hellerstein, "Neuroplasticity and Depression," *Psychology Today*, July 14, 2011, www.psychologytoday.com/us/blog/heal -your-brain/201107/neuroplasticity-and-depression.

11. Rebekah Lyons, *Rhythms of Renewal: Trading Stress and Anxiety for a Life of Peace and Purpose* (Grand Rapids: Zondervan, 2019), 21–22.

12. See Thompson, *Soul of Desire*, 127.

Rule 4: Make Meaning

1. Clay Routledge, "Suicides Have Increased. Is This an Existential Crisis?" *New York Times*, June 23, 2018, www.nytimes.com/2018/06/23/opinion/sunday/suicide-rate-existential-crisis.html.

Chapter 13: Follow the Longing

1. Saint Augustine, *Confessions*, trans. Henry Chadwick (Oxford: Oxford University Press, 1991), 3.

2. N. T. Wright, *Simply Christian: Why Christianity Makes Sense* (San Francisco: HarperSanFrancisco, 2006), 9, italics in original.

3. Timothy D. Willard, *The Beauty Chasers: Recapturing the Wonder of the Divine* (Grand Rapids: Zondervan, 2022), 41, italics in original.

4. See Curt Thompson, *The Soul of Desire: Discovering the Neuroscience of Longing, Beauty, and Community* (Downers Grove, IL: IVP, 2021), 10–16.

Chapter 14: Create Flourishing Spaces

1. Douglas McKelvey, "Liturgies of Blessing and Celebration: To Mark the First Hearthfire of the Season," in *Every Moment Holy*, vol. 1 (Nashville: Rabbit Room, 2017), 119.

2. Michelle Dozois, "5 Cheap(ish) Things to Help You Have a Very 'Hygge' Winter," *New York Times*, December 12, 2017, www.nytimes.com/2017/12/07/smarter-living/5-cheap-ish-things-to-help-you-have-a-very-hygge-winter.html.

3. We've enjoyed the ARO box product and companion app that tracks the amount of time we've intentionally put our devices down, encouraging us to do something more creative with our time. For more information, go to www.goaro.com.

4. See Emily G. Johnson et al., "The Effectiveness of Trauma-Informed Wilderness Therapy with Adolescents: A Pilot Study," *Psychological Trauma* 12, no. 8 (November 2020): 878–87, https://pubmed.ncbi.nlm.nih.gov/32496098.

5. See "Should My Spouse and I Attend a Marriage Intensive or Retreat?" WinShape Marriage, April 29, 2022, https://marriage .winshape.org/resource/intensive-or-retreat. The WinShape retreats include everything from ropes course experiences to adventure trips with other couples.

Chapter 15: Make Good Things

1. Viktor Frankl, *Man's Search for Meaning* (Boston: Beacon, 1959), 169.
2. Judah and the Lion, "Help Me to Feel Again," Cletus the Van Records, 2021.
3. See Michael Metzger, "Living the Gospel in Culture," Ideas for the Common Good, http://208.106.253.109/essays/living-the-gospel -in-culture.aspx?page=3, accessed November 11, 2022.
4. Charles Colson and Nancy Pearcey, *How Now Shall We Live?* (Carol Stream, IL: Tyndale, 1999), xii.
5. Rebekah Lyons, *Freefall to Fly: A Breathtaking Journey toward a Life of Meaning* (Carol Stream, IL: Tyndale, 2013).
6. See Valeria Sabater, "Working with Your Hands Is Good for Your Brain," Exploring Your Mind, November 15, 2021, https://exploringyourmind.com/working-with-your-hands -is-good-for-your-brain, accessed November 11, 2022.
7. See Kelly Lambert, *Lifting Depression: A Neuroscientist's Hands-on Approach to Activating Your Brain's Healing Power* (New York: Basic Books, 2010); see Sabater, "Working with Your Hands."
8. Sabater, "Working with Your Hands."
9. Rory Groves, *Durable Trades: Family-Centered Economies That Have Stood the Test of Time* (Eugene, OR: Wipf & Stock, 2020), xvii–xviii.

Rule 5: Endure Together

1. Michael S. Erwin and Willys DeVoll, *Leadership Is a Relationship: How to Put People First in the Digital World* (Hoboken, NJ: Wiley, 2021), 45.

Chapter 16: Link Arms, Join Hearts

1. Cynthia Cox, "Mental Illnesses May Soon Be the Most Common Pre-existing Conditions," Kaiser Family Foundation, October 8,

2020, www.kff.org/policy-watch/mental-illness-may-soon-be
-most-common-pre-existing-conditions.

2. Olufunke M. Benson and Melissa L. Whitson, "The Protective
Role of Sense of Community and Access to Resources on College
Student Stress and COVID-19-Related Daily Life Disruptions,"
Journal of Community Psychology 50, no. 6 (August 2022): 2746–64,
https://onlinelibrary.wiley.com/doi/10.1002/jcop.22817.

3. Benson and Whitson, "Protective Role of Sense of Community."

4. See "Building Your Resilience," American Psychological
Association, January 1, 2012 (last updated February 1, 2020),
www.apa.org/topics/resilience/building-your-resilience.

5. See Charles E. Fritz, "Disasters and Mental Health: Therapeutic
Principles Drawn from Disaster Studies," University of Delaware
Research Center (Historical and Comparative Disaster Series #10;
1996), https://udspace.udel.edu/bitstream/handle/19716/1325
/HC%2010.pdf, accessed October 29, 2022, italics added.

6. Fritz, "Disasters and Mental Health."

Chapter 17: Build Small and Strong

1. Sebastian Junger, *Tribe: On Homecoming and Belonging* (New York:
Twelve, 2016), 109.

2. See Donald B. Kraybill, "Lessons from the Amish," Q Ideas
Culture Summit, April 2022.

Chapter 18: Harness the Power of We

1. Blaise Pascal wrote about "the wager" in his book *Pensées*, first
published in 1670.

2. N. T. Wright, *Simply Christian: Why Christianity Makes Sense*
(San Francisco: HarperSanFrancisco, 2006), 210, italics in original.

3. "Create Community: Community Health Resilience,"
CDC Center for Preparedness and Response, www.cdc.gov
/prepyourhealth/createcommunity/index.htm, italics added.

RHYTHMS FOR LIFE PODCAST

Join Rebekah & Gabe for conversations with experts and access free resources to build resilience in your emotional, spiritual and relational health.

RHYTHMS OF RENEWAL

Trading Stress and Anxiety for a Life of Peace and Purpose

DISCOVER HOW TO:

- Take charge of your emotional health & invite others to do the same.
- Overcome anxiety with daily habits that strengthen you mentally.
- Find joy through restored realtionships in your family & community.
- Walk in confidence with the unique gifts you have to offer the world.

Available in stores and online!

A SURRENDERED YES

52 Devotionals to Let Go
and Live Free

DISCOVER HOW TO:

- Find freedom from the approval of others.

- Use your time and energy to live a life of intention.

- Practice rhythms for emotional, physical, and spiritual health.

- Release control to find God's presence in play and laughter.

Available in stores and online!

YOU ARE FREE

Be Who You Already Are

BE INSPIRED TO:

- Overcome exhaustion of people pleasing & rest in God's freedom.

- Release stress and anxiety to uncover the peace of God's presence.

- Find permission to grieve past disappointments & encounter healing.

- Discover the courage to use your newfound freedom to set others free.

Available in stores and online!

FREEFALL TO FLY

A Breathtaking Journey to a Life of Meaning

REBEKAH INVITES YOU TO:

- Remember you're not alone in this journey towards wholeness.
- Revisit dreams birthed in your childhoood & uncover purpose.
- Allow your God-given talents and burdens to emerge with meaning.
- Find the courage to face your fears, and encounter transformation.

Available in stores and online!

Go Deeper with the Companion Video Study

Study Guide plus Streaming
Video 9780310149323

DVD
025986149345

Available now at your favorite bookstore,
or streaming video on StudyGateway.com.

From the Publisher

GREAT BOOKS

ARE EVEN BETTER WHEN THEY'RE SHARED!

Help other readers find this one:

- Post a review at your favorite online bookseller

- Post a picture on a social media account and share why you enjoyed it

- Send a note to a friend who would also love it—or better yet, give them a copy

Thanks for reading!